P9-DIJ-738

6
AGES 11-12

SCORE!

Mountain Challenge

LANGUAGE ARTS WORKBOOK

KAPLAN

PUBLISHING

New York

Contributing Editor: Justin Serrano
Editorial Director: Jennifer Farthing
Editorial Development Manager: Tonya Lobato
Assistant Editor: Eric Titner
Production Editor: Dominique Polfliet
Production Artist: Creative Pages, Inc.
Cover Designer: Carly Schnur

© 2007 by Kaplan, Inc.

Published by Kaplan Publishing, a division of Kaplan, Inc.
888 Seventh Ave.
New York, NY 10106

Printed in the United States of America

May 2007
10 9 8 7 6 5 4 3 2 1

ISBN-13: 978-1-4195-9464-9
ISBN-10: 1-4195-9464-8

Kaplan Publishing books are available at special quantity discounts to use for sales promotions, employee premiums, or educational purposes. Please email our Special Sales Department to order or for more information at *kaplanpublishing@kaplan.com*, or write to Kaplan Publishing, 888 Seventh Avenue, 22nd Floor, New York, NY 10106.

Table of Contents

Are you ready for a fun and challenging trip up *SCORE!* Mountain?

Getting Started

This exciting, interactive workbook will guide you through 6 unique base camps as you make your way up *SCORE!* Mountain. Along the way to the top you will have the opportunity to challenge yourself with over 150 language arts questions, activities, and brain busters as you work towards conquering *SCORE!* Mountain.

To help you figure out the answer to each question, use the blank space on the page or the extra pages at the back of your workbook. If you need extra space, use a piece of scrap paper.

Base Camp

SCORE! Mountain is divided into 6 base camps—each covering an essential language arts topic—and is aligned to the educational standards set forth by the National Council of Teachers of English. The final base camp in this workbook, Everyday Writing, has a special focus on the many ways we might use writing each day.

Your trip through base camp will take you through 19 questions related to the base camp topic, a Challenge Activity designed to give your brain an extra workout, and a 5-question test to see how much you've learned during your climb.

Each question comes with helpful hints to guide you to the right answer. Use these hints to make your climb up *SCORE!* Mountain a successful learning experience!

The Answer Hider

We encourage you to give each question your best effort before looking at the answer; that's why your *SCORE! Mountain Challenge Workbook* comes equipped with a handy answer hider. Tear out the answer hider and, while you work on each question, use your answer hider to cover up the solution until you're finished. Then, uncover the answer and see how well you did!

Celebrate!

At the end of each base camp, there's a fun celebration as a reward for successfully making it through. It's the perfect opportunity to take a break and refresh yourself before tackling the next base camp!

SCORE! Mountain Challenge Online Companion

Don't forget—more fun awaits you online! Each base camp comes with a set of 10 online questions and interactive activities, plus a mountain-climbing study partner who will encourage you and help you track your progress as you get closer to the top of *SCORE!* Mountain!

SCORE! online base camps are designed to supplement the educational themes of each base camp from the workbook. As you reach the end of each base camp in the workbook, we encourage you to go to your computer to round out your *SCORE!* Mountain Challenge experience. PLUS, after you successfully complete the last online base camp you are awarded a Certificate of Achievement.

Certificate of Achievement

Upon completion of the entire workbook and online program, you will receive your very own Certificate of Achievement that can be shared with family and friends!

Time Management

In addition to all of the great language arts practice that your *SCORE! Mountain Challenge Workbook* has to offer, you'll find an array of helpful tips and strategies at the front of the workbook on how you can best organize and manage your time to stay on top of your busy schedule, do well at school, get all of your homework and chores done, and still have time for fun, family, and friends! It's a great way to help you perform at your best every day!

Tools

Every mountain climber needs a set of tools to help him or her reach the mountaintop! Your *SCORE! Mountain Challenge Workbook* has a special set of tools for you. In the back of your workbook you'll find a handy guide to help you get through each base camp. Turn to the back of the workbook and use these tools whenever you need a helping hand during your climb up *SCORE!* Mountain.

Enjoy your trip up *SCORE!* Mountain. We hope that it's a fun and educational learning experience!

GOOD LUCK!

Being organized and managing your time well are very important skills to learn. It's a valuable key to success!

Here are some tips to help.

Getting Started

- *Be realistic.* We all wish that we had an endless number of hours in the day to take care of all our responsibilities and still have time for all of the fun things we want to do. The truth is that every person in the world has the same amount of time to work with. Each of us gets 24 hours a day, 7 days a week, so how you budget your time is important!

- *Keep a schedule.* To help you keep track of your time, try creating a weekly schedule. You can use a calendar or organizer, or you can make your own schedule on a blank piece of paper. Your weekly schedule might look similar to the one below.

My Weekly Schedule

	MON.	TUES.	WED.	THURS.	FRI.	SAT.	SUN.
6:00 A.M.							
7:00 A.M.							
8:00 A.M.							
9:00 A.M.							
10:00 A.M.							
11:00 A.M.							
12:00 A.M.							
1:00 P.M.							
2:00 P.M.							
3:00 P.M.							
4:00 P.M.							
5:00 P.M.							
6:00 P.M.							
7:00 P.M.							
8:00 P.M.							
9:00 P.M.							
10:00 P.M.							

- *Budget time.* Set aside time on your schedule for all of your regular daily activities. For instance, if you go to school between 7:00 A.M. and 2:30 P.M. each weekday, write that on your schedule. Be sure to include any important chores, responsibilities, after-school clubs, and special events. Budget time for homework and school assignments as well, but also make time for fun with your friends and family!

Staying Organized:

- *Write it down.* The best way to keep track of new activities or assignments is to write them down. Whenever something new comes up, add it to your schedule!

  You can also try keeping a "To Do" list to make sure you remember everything. Try to estimate the amount of time it will take to complete your assignments. It's a good way to budget your time!

- *Have a daily plan.* Each day, plan out what chores, assignments, and activities you have to do that day. Use your "To Do" list to help. Some activities may take up more time, so make sure you have enough time that day to complete everything. Your daily plan might look similar to the one below.

Sample Daily Plan

MONDAY	
6:00 A.M.	Get up, get dressed
7:00 A.M.	Eat breakfast Go to school
7:40 A.M.	School starts
2:30 P.M.	School ends Karate Club meeting – gym
3:30 P.M.	Get home from school
4:00 P.M.	Homework, and chores (see "To Do" list)
6:30 P.M.	Dinner
7:30 P.M.	Call friends and watch TV
8:45 P.M.	Get ready for bed
9:00 P.M.	Bed

Doing Homework

- *Set homework time.* Your schedule should include a block of time for doing homework. If possible, make this block of time for right after school is finished, so you're sure to have enough time to complete your assignments. How much time do you usually need for homework? Write that on your weekly schedule.

- *Get right to it!* When it's time to do your homework, stay focused. Try to work straight through until you get it done. You'll be happy to finish, so you can move on to other fun things! Sometimes a small, healthful snack can help keep you going and energized!

- *Stay organized.* Set up your homework space in a well-lit area with all the things you'll need to do a great job. This includes your schoolbooks, a dictionary, a calculator, pens, and extra paper. If you keep these items handy, it makes learning a lot more organized and fun!

- *Improve your skills.* Good students develop their skills both inside and outside the classroom. Your *SCORE! Mountain Challenge Workbook* can help. Set aside part of your homework time each day for completing sections from the workbook. Check your progress with the online quizzes as well.

Chores and Activities

- *Keep your commitments.* Remember to include your chores in your daily schedule. You might even set aside a "chore time." Be sure to include chores on your daily "To Do" list as well.

- *Know your limits.* How many school activities can you manage? Be realistic when you join clubs or sign up for activities. Activities are fun, but you must make time for all of the other things going on in your life.

- *Set priorities.* If you don't have many commitments, you can get everything done in your free time. But what if you're committed to more things than you have time for? Then you must set priorities.

  A **priority** is something that's important to you. When you set priorities, you choose the items from your list that are most important to complete.

Use the worksheet below to help you determine your priorities.

Priorities Worksheet

Review the list of activities below. Write your own activities in the blank spaces next to Clubs, Classes, and Sports. Add any other activities on the lines next to Other.

In the column marked Priority, give each activity a letter: **A**, **B**, or **C**:

- **Priority A** = very important to me
- **Priority B** = important to me
- **Priority C** = less important to me

Priority	Activity	Priority	Activity
_____	Homework _____	_____	Sports _____
	_____	_____	_____
_____	Chores _____		
_____	_____	_____	Other _____
_____	Clubs _____	_____	_____
_____	_____	_____	_____
_____	Classes _____	_____	_____
_____	_____	_____	_____

List your top 5 priorities below. These items are the most important to you. You should always focus on getting these done.

Priority	Activity
1	
2	
3	
4	
5	

Once you know what's important to you, make sure the things that are top priority get done first!

Setting Goals

- **Even though you're busy, it's also great to try new things.** Setting goals will help you with this!

- Do you want to try a new sport, join a new club at school, or read a new book? Fill in the spaces below to help you start reaching your goals. Every time you reach a goal, make a new goal for yourself. You'll be amazed at how much you can do!

What is your #1 goal?

_____

_____

How are you going to reach your #1 goal?

_____

_____

Leaving Time for Fun!

- Everyone needs time to relax and recharge. Include some time in your schedule for relaxing and just having fun with your family and friends. You'll be glad you did!

Your *SCORE! Mountain Challenge Workbook* comes with a fun, interactive online companion. Parents, go online to register your child at **kaptest.com/scorebooksonline**. Here your child can access 60 exciting language arts activities and a cool mountain-climbing study partner.

Children, when you log on, you'll be brought to a page where you will find your *SCORE! Mountain Challenge Workbook* cover. You'll also be asked for a **password**, which you will get from a passage in this workbook. So have your workbook handy when you're ready to continue your *SCORE!* Mountain Challenge online, and follow the directions.

Good luck and have fun climbing!

Read the passage below, then answer questions 1 and 2.

Mr. Phileas Fogg lived, in 1872, at No. 7, Saville Row, Burlington Gardens, the house in which Sheridan died in 1814. He was one of the most noticeable members of the Reform Club, though he seemed always to avoid attracting attention; an *enigmatical* personage, about whom little was known, except that he was a *polished* man of the world. People said that he resembled Byron—at least that his head was Byronic; but he was a bearded, tranquil Byron, who might live on a thousand years without growing old.

–from *Around the World in 80 Days*, by Jules Verne

1. Based on how it's used in the passage, what does the word *enigmatical* probably mean?

   Mysterious

Hint #1:

Look for **context clues** in the passage that will help you figure out what this word means. The next phrase in the sentence is "**about whom little was known.**" That tells you something about Mr. Fogg, too: that people didn't know him very well.

Hint #2:

This word is based on the word *enigma*. Some things that people describe as enigmas are **unsolved crimes** and **the pyramids in Egypt**. Does this information give you a clue as to what *enigmatical* means?

Answer: *Enigmatical* means **mysterious**, like a riddle. An enigmatical person is someone who is hard to get to know.

© Kaplan Publishing, Inc.

2. As it is used in the passage, what does the word *polished* most **likely** mean? Circle your answer.

(A) shiny

(B) practiced

(C) sophisticated

(D) rough

Hint #1:

Phineas Fogg, aside from having a unique name, is described as a "**man of the world**." What does that mean to you?

Hint #2:

This is one of those words that can have **more than one meaning**. Make sure to choose the meaning that **best** matches the way the word is used in this passage.

Answer: Choice **C** is correct.

When the passage refers to Mr. Fogg as being "a polished man of the world," he is being described as **sophisticated**.

3. The *Zygocactus*, or **Christmas cactus**, is so named because it flowers at an _____ time of year when, in many places, nothing else is in bloom.

Choose the word that **best** fits into the blank space above.

(A) expected

(B) unlikely

(C) unappealing

(D) ugly

Hint #1:

Would you expect a plant to flower at Christmas? Unless you live in a southern state or the southern hemisphere, probably not!

Hint #2:

Most people are happy to see flowers.

Answer: Choice **B** is correct.

During December, plants in many parts of the world are **not** flowering. The fact that the Christmas cactus flowers in December is a nice thing and a surprising one, too. The word that best matches this idea is **unlikely**.

Read the sentence below, then answer questions 4 and 5.

The musician was *skilled* at playing her guitar; her fingers practically flew over the strings.

4. What is a **synonym** for the word *skilled*?

Advanced, and talented

Hint #1:

In case you didn't remember, a **synonym** is a word that means almost, or even exactly, the **same thing** as another word.

Hint #2:

If you know what the word *skill* means, you could try to think of a synonym for it, and then add "**-ed**" to the end of that word.

Answer: There are several synonyms for the word *skilled*.

Some answers include: **talented**, **practiced**, and **accomplished**.

© Kaplan Publishing, Inc.

5. Saying that the musician's fingers **"practically flew"** is an example of what?

Ⓐ simple language

Ⓑ foreign language

Ⓒ confusing language

Ⓓ figurative language

Hint #1:

Did the musician's fingers actually fly? Come to think of it, can fingers actually fly at all?

Hint #2:

What do you see in your head when you read this sentence?

Answer: Choice **D** is correct.

The writer is describing the musician, using images rather than direct words. He could have said, "Her hands moved quickly," but instead he said that they **"practically flew."** This is an example of **figurative language**.

6. Use the words below to make a **simile**.

souffle

feather

the souffle is as light
as a feather.

Hint #1:

A **souffle** is a very airy food that puffs up when it bakes.

Hint #2:

Similes are comparisons that use the words *like* or *as*. For example, "**Your bedroom is as clean as the dump**."

Answer: The souffle was as light as a feather.

A souffle is a very **light** food, and feathers are **lightweight**. Things that don't weigh much are often referred to as being "**as light as a feather.**"

Your simile may be a little bit different, but that's okay. As long as you compared the souffle and feather using the words *like* or *as*, then you're on the right track!

7. For the following word, think of **one synonym** and **one antonym**, then write each word on the lines provided.

brave

synonym: *coreagus*

antonym: *cowardry*

Hint #1:

Heroes, soldiers, and firefighters are described as being **brave**.

Hint #2:

Someone who is **not brave** is probably **easily scared**.

Answer: There are several synonyms and antonyms that you can come up with for the word **brave**.

Some **synonyms** include: **courageous**, **daring**, **bold**, and **fearless**.

Some **antonyms** include: **cowardly**, **scared**, **fearful**, and **timid**.

Remember, a **synonym** of a word should mean about the same thing as the original word. An **antonym** should mean about the opposite.

Read the poem below, then answer question 8 on the following page.

Bed in Summer

In winter I get up at night
And dress by yellow candlelight.
In summer quite the other way,
I have to go to bed by day.

I have to go to bed and see
The birds still hopping on the tree,
Or hear the grown-up people's feet
Still going past me in the street.

And does it not seem hard to you,
When all the sky is clear and blue,
And I should like so much to play,
To have to go to bed by day?

–from *A Child's Garden of Verses*, by Robert Louis Stevenson

8. What does the narrator mean when he says, "I have to go to bed by day"?

It is still Light out when he goes to sleep.

Hint #1:

The narrator in this poem is a little kid.

Hint #2:

Besides the weather, how else are summer days and winter days different?

Answer: During the summer it isn't even dark yet when he has to go to bed, which is why he says, "I have to go to bed by day." The sun sets **later** during the summer than it does during the winter. The narrator is a child who has to go to bed early and get up early.

9. Fill in the blank in the sentence below.

The difference in meaning between *behave*
and *misbehave* is that *misbehave* means ___Dis obey___.
not to obey

Hint #1:

What other words start with the prefix **mis-**?

Hint #2:

Has anyone ever told you that you were **misbehaving**? What were you doing when you were told that?

Answer: *Misbehave* means **not to behave**. The prefix *mis-* means **not**, so when it is added to the beginning of a word, it changes the meaning of the word to its **opposite**.

10. What prefix can you put in front of the word *interested* to mean **not interested**?

    Ⓐ pre-

    Ⓑ inter-

    Ⓒ dis-

    Ⓓ sub-

Hint #1:

Think of words you know that start with the letters in each of the choices. Which ones seem to mean **not** in some way?

Hint #2:

Attach each answer choice to the word ***interested*** and try saying each possible new version of the word to yourself. Which one sounds best to your ear?

Answer: Choice **C** is correct.

Disinterested means **not interested.**

11. What is the difference in meaning between *adventurous* and *reckless*?

they each have
other feelings, reckless is negitive

Hint #1:

One of these words has a more **negative** feeling than the other. Can you tell which one?

Hint #2:

Have you used these words before? In what **context** have you used each of them?

Answer: *Adventurous* means having the desire to try new things. Someone who is *reckless* takes being adventurous to an irresponsible extreme. Someone who is reckless also **does not think about the risks or dangers involved** in trying those new things.

12. Which one of these **suffixes** would change the word *quiet* to an adverb?

(A) -ness

(B) -ly

(C) -er

(D) -or

Hint #1:

Do you remember what an **adverb** is? It's like an adjective, except that it **modifies a verb** instead of a noun.

Hint #2:

Most adverbs have the **same ending**. Can you remember what that is? Think of some other adverbs to see if that helps.

Answer: Choice **B** is correct.

Look at the sentence, "Doug spoke **quietly** in the library." *Quietly* is an **adverb** that modifies the verb *spoke*. Most adverbs end in **-ly**.

Read the passage below and then answer questions 13–16.

If I were to sell the reader a barrel of molasses, and he, instead of sweetening his substantial dinner with the same at judicious intervals, should eat the entire barrel at one sitting, and then abuse me for making him sick, I would say that he deserved to be made sick for not knowing any better how to utilize the blessings this world affords. And if I sell to the reader this volume of nonsense, and he, instead of seasoning his graver reading with a chapter of it now and then, when his mind demands such relaxation, unwisely overdoses himself with several chapters of it at a single sitting, he will deserve to be nauseated . . . . It lies wholly with the customer whether he will injure himself by means of either, or will derive from them the benefits which they will *afford* him if he uses their possibilities *judiciously*.

–from the preface to the English edition of *Mark Twain's Sketches*

13. The author uses the description of the **"barrel of molasses"** as a kind of

Ⓐ hyperbole.

Ⓑ assonance.

Ⓒ personification.

Ⓓ metaphor.

Hint #1:

The author is **comparing** the way people read his books with the way they might use a barrel of molasses.

Hint #2:

The author isn't actually saying that anyone eats an entire barrel of molasses in one sitting. It's a way of helping the reader better understand the point he is trying to make.

Answer: Choice **D** is correct.

In the passage, the author is **comparing** the way people read his books with the way they might use a barrel of molasses. The author uses the description of the **"barrel of molasses"** as a **metaphor**, which is a way to compare two things.

14. As it is used in last sentence of the passage, what does the word *afford* mean?

(A) provide

(B) allow

(C) pay for

(D) has the money for

© Kaplan Publishing, Inc.

Hint #1:

The word *afford* can have different meanings, depending on how it's used.

Hint #2:

Are blessings something you would expect to have to pay for?

Answer: Choice **A** is correct.

According to the passage, the world is **offering**, or **providing**, certain blessings, but people must figure out how to use those gifts.

15. Based on the way it is used in the passage, which of the following words would be the best synonym for *judiciously*?

Ⓐ crazily

Ⓑ wisely

Ⓒ happily

Ⓓ carelessly

Hint #1:

The words *judiciously* and *judge* share the **same root**. Which word best matches how a judge must act?

Hint #2:

During this passage, how has the author been **encouraging** people to act, both with the molasses and with the book?

Answer: Choice **B** is correct.

Judiciously means **intelligently** or **sensibly**, so the best match would be choice **B**. The author has been telling people that it's up to them to control themselves. If, in one sitting, they eat an entire barrel of molasses, read his entire book, or eat a whole candy store, it's their fault, not his.

16. Based on what you now know about the word *judiciously*, think of an **antonym** for it.

antonym: ___foolishness___

judiciously

Hint #1:

From the previous question, you now know that ***judiciously*** means **wisely**.

Hint #2:

Remember, **antonyms** are words that are nearly **opposite** in meaning to other words.

Answer: There are several different antonyms that you can come up with for the word **judiciously**.

Some possible **antonyms** include: **foolishly**, **stupidly**, **thoughtlessly**, or **unwisely**.

17. Underline the examples of **onomatopoeia** in the sentences below.

The bee stopped buzzing when it heard the familiar hiss. The frog splashed into the water and swam away. "No one likes me," mumbled the snake as it slithered past.

Hint #1:

Onomatopoeia is using a word that **sounds like the sound it represents**.

Hint #2:

Try reading the sentences out loud. What words sound like the sounds they represent?

Answer: The bee stopped **buzzing** when it heard the familiar **hiss**. The frog **splashed** into the water and swam away. "No one likes me," **mumbled** the snake as it **slithered** past.

18. Based on how *loping* and *clambered* are used in the sentence below, how do you think both words are related in meaning?

When he realized he would miss dessert, Jeffrey stopped **loping** along and **clambered** up the steep hill back home.

Both mean walking But in diffrent ways.

Hint #1:

Jeffrey changed the way he was moving when he realized he would miss dessert. Most people like dessert, so he probably wanted to get it as quick as he could.

Hint #2:

How might you get up a steep hill if you were in a hurry?

Answer: Both words mean **walking**, but in different ways.

Loping means **moving slowly, in a relaxed way**.

Clambering means **moving quickly and awkwardly, climbing with both your hands and your feet**.

19. Look at the words below:

international   **interact**   **intersection**

What does the prefix *inter-* probably mean?

act with out between

© Kaplan Publishing, Inc.

Hint #1:

Think about what each of these words mean. Can you find anything **in common** among their definitions?

Hint #2:

The Olympics are an international event.

Answer: Inter- means **between** or **among**.

Something **international** happens between two or more nations.

An **intersection** is a cross of two or more streets or lines.

You need two or more people to **interact**, because *interaction* means **talking to each other** or **cooperating**.

Challenge Activity

You're doing a great job so far!
Are you ready for a Challenge Activity?

Good luck!

Read the paragraph below, then answer the questions that follow.

Before the big, blue *barge* came to a stop along the long, hot dock, the anchor brushed itself off, ready to dive to the bottom of the water, and the rope got fit to be tied about its job. The deck creaked, the engine whirred, and the wheel spun. The captain raised his hat and declared, "We're swimming in success, gentlemen!" His exclamation could be heard around the whole world, and the sun peeked out from behind a cloud like a child eager to eavesdrop on a party. Standing on the deck, Myrtle turned to Juniper and winked. "Well you know, a bird in the hand is worth two in the bush." Juniper turned with a *spreading* grin, "Break a leg, dear."

a) On the lines below, list every example of figurative language you can find in this paragraph.

Alliteration: _____

Assonance: _____

Cliché: _____

Hyperbole: _____

Idiom: _____

Metaphor: _____

Onomatopoeia: _____

Personification: _____

Simile: _____

© Kaplan Publishing, Inc.

b) Based on how it's used in the passage, what is the **best** meaning for the word *barge*?

(A) crash

(B) boat

(C) painting

(D) bird

c) As it is used in the passage, name one **synonym** and one **antonym** for the word *spreading*.

synonym: _____

antonym: _____

Hint #1:

Use the list of definitions below to help you recognize each type of figurative language.

Alliteration: A device that repeats the same beginning word sound for effect

Assonance: The repetition of vowel sounds within a short passage of verse or prose

Cliché: A phrase, expression, or idea that has been overused to the point of losing its intended force or novelty

Hyperbole: An exaggeration used for emphasis

Idiom: A word or phrase with a figurative meaning that is known only through conventional use, not from the literal definition

Metaphor: A comparison that does not use the words *like* or *as*

Onomatopoeia: A word that sounds like the sound it represents

Personification: Giving human characteristics to nonhuman things

Simile: A comparison using the words *like* or *as*

See hint and answers on following page.

Hint #2:

Juniper's grin is **spreading** as he talks to Myrtle. Does he seem to be getting happier or sadder?

Answers to Challenge Activity:

a) Did you find all the examples of figurative language in the paragraph?

Alliteration: <u>before, big, blue, barge</u>
Assonance: <u>along, long; hot, dock</u>
Cliché: <u>a bird in the hand is worth two in the bush</u>
Hyperbole: <u>his exclamation could be heard around the whole world</u>
Idiom: <u>fit to be tied, break a leg</u>
Metaphor: <u>we're swimming in success</u>
Onomatopoeia: <u>creaked, whirred</u>
Personification: <u>sail lazily stopped, anchor brushed itself off, rope got fit to be tied</u>
Simile: <u>sun peeked out from behind a cloud like a child eager to eavesdrop on a party</u>

b) Choice **B** is correct.
Based on how it's used in the passage, the **best** meaning for *barge* is a **boat**.

c) There are many possible synonyms and antonyms for the word spreading. Here are some examples:
Synonyms: <u>unfolding</u> or <u>growing</u>
Antonym: <u>disappearing</u> or <u>shrinking</u>

© Kaplan Publishing, Inc.

Test

Let's take a quick test and see how much you've learned during this climb up *SCORE!* Mountain.

Good luck!

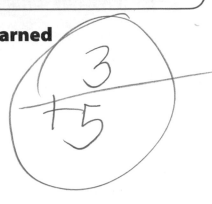

1. Which of the following means "more sleepy"?

   (A) sleeper

   (B) sleepiest

   (C) sleepily

   (D) sleepier

2. Read the sentence below. What does the word *hone* probably mean?

   After the sculptor had removed the large pieces of stone, she began to **hone** the image of the subject's face.

   (A) break

   (B) sketch

   (C) improve

   (D) change

Read the following poem, then answer questions 3–5.

The beautiful leaves fall over and over,
They spin and drop to the earth,
Covering the ground like a big brown blanket.

The trees left bare,
Shivering wood against the cold,
Pining through winter for a new coat.

Spring soon comes,
As do the happy feet of dancing flowers,
And happiness returns,
And fills the hours.

3. The **first stanza** of this poem is an example of

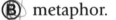 **(A)** simile.

(B) metaphor.

(C) onomatopoeia.

(D) alliteration.

4. Based on how it is used in the poem, what does the word *pining* most likely mean?

(A) to hibernate

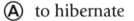 **(B)** to long for

(C) to freeze

(D) to stand

5. The phrase "the happy feet of dancing flowers" is an example of

(A) idiom.

(B) cliché.

(C) assonance.

(D) personification.

Answers to test questions:

1. Choice **D** is correct.
Sleepier means more sleepy.

2. Choice **C** is correct.
Hone means **to improve**. The sculptor is working on improving the image of the subject's face in the stone.

3. Choice **A** is correct.
The first stanza of the poem is an example of **simile**. The falling leaves are described as covering the earth "like a big brown blanket."

4. Choice **B** is correct.
Based on how it is used in the poem, the word *pining* means **to long for**. In the poem, the trees are left bare in the winter and long for a new coat of leaves to protect them from the cold.

5. Choice **D** is correct.
"The happy feet of dancing flowers" is an example of **personification**. The author's choice of words gives the flowers the human characteristic of dancing.

Celebrate!

Let's take a fun break before we go to the next base camp. You've earned it!

Let's have some fun reading something you like!

Take some time out to read a chapter from a favorite book, an article from your local newspaper or magazine, or whatever you like—it's your choice!

Congratulations!

You're on your way up *SCORE!* Mountain.

BASE CAMP 1

Better yet, take a trip and visit your local or school library and check out a few of your favorites!

Take a break, expand your mind, and let your imagination and thoughts wander through the pages of your favorite reading material!

Good luck and have fun!
You deserve it for working so hard!

Read the passage below, then answer questions 1–4.

Plants need to be repotted as they grow. Follow these directions to repot your plants with ease:

- Place a hand on the top of the soil and tip the whole pot on its side, then nearly upside down, so that the whole plant, including the roots and soil, dislodges from the pot.

- With your free hand, carefully loosen the soil around the roots.

- Fill the new pot about halfway with soil.

- Set the plant in the new pot, on the new soil.

- Pour more soil into the pot so that there are no empty areas around the plant.

- Gently pat down the soil all around the plant.

- Water the plant; use plant food only if the soil doesn't already contain food.

1. Which of the following would be the **best title** for this passage?

   Ⓐ How to Repot Household Plants

   Ⓑ Common Plant Care Questions

   Ⓒ Best Plants for Low Light Conditions

   Ⓓ Breaking Up the Root Structure

Hint #1:

What is this passage about? Try to say it in **one sentence**; that will give you a good idea of what the title should be.

Hint #2:

The title should sum up the information about the **whole passage**. If any of the titles are about details from the passage, eliminate them!

Answer: Choice **A** is correct.

How to Repot Household Plants would be a good title for this passage, because the instructions describe how to repot any household plant. The passage is specifically about repotting plants, so any title that talks about plants in general, or anything else specific to plants, is wrong.

© Kaplan Publishing, Inc.

2. The instructions given in the passage would **not** work when repotting

- Ⓐ a very small plant.
- Ⓑ more than one plant on the same day.
- Ⓒ a cactus.
- Ⓓ someone else's plant.

© Kaplan Publishing, Inc.

Hint #1:

Think about each of these situations. What problems could someone encounter in each one?

Hint #2:

Reread the instructions on how to repot household plants to refresh your memory.

Answer: Choice **C** is correct.

A **cactus** is prickly and hard to hold. For repotting a cactus, the instructions would probably need to mention wearing heavy gloves to protect your hands.

3. What instruction could the author add at the **beginning** of the passage to make it **clearer**?

(A) Place your plant in a sunny spot.

(B) Be sure to have a larger pot and potting soil handy.

(C) You can use a special tool to break apart the roots.

(D) Some soil contains plant food.

Hint #1:

A new instruction at the beginning should be useful at the very **beginning** of performing the action being discussed.

Hint #2:

What might someone forget to do **before** they start repotting a plant?

Answer: Choice **B** is correct.

A new instruction should be added at the beginning to cover a task that needs to happen **before** everything else. The one thing that the instructions don't mention is what **supplies** you should have on hand to repot a plant. It would be helpful to have a larger pot and potting soil handy.

4. In what situation should you **not** add plant food to the water?

_____

_____

_____

_____

© Kaplan Publishing, Inc.

Hint #1:

Where in the instructions does the author talk about plant food? Look for that place, and you'll probably find some helpful information.

Hint #2:

Plant food is usually good for plants, but when would adding it be a bad idea?

Answer: You should not add plant food to the water **when the soil already contains plant food**. The instructions say to give the plant food when watering it only if the soil doesn't already contain food. If it does, you might give the plant too much food and hurt it.

Read the passage below, then answer questions 5 and 6.

True mollusks come in two main varieties: **bivalves** and **univalves**. Bivalves have two shells, fitting together along a toothed hinge on one side and kept closed by means of adductor muscles. Univalves have only one shell, usually coiled, but sometimes shaped like a cap or miniature volcano. Some marine univalves can seal themselves inside their shells with something called an operculum, which covers the open end of the shell like a trap door. Although mollusks take on many different shapes, they are much alike inside. Each has a foot, a breathing siphon, a tiny brain and heart, and a fleshy mantle, which produces lime for shell building. Most true mollusks have eyes, but a few are blind. Many have teeth, called radulae.

5. The author's **purpose** for writing this passage is to

Ⓐ convince readers to protect mollusks from extinction.

Ⓑ describe the bodies of most mollusks.

Ⓒ share an emotional personal experience.

Ⓓ defend how much better mollusks see than humans.

Hint #1:

This passage sounds as though it came from a science textbook. Which answer choice sounds like a science textbook?

Hint #2:

Does this passage sound emotional or not?

Answer: Choice **B** is correct.

This passage is written like a science textbook. Textbooks are usually written to be **unemotional** and **fair**. They don't try to convince readers of anything, and they are **not** personal. The only choice that isn't emotional or personal in some way is choice B. The author's purpose for writing this passage is to **describe the bodies of most mollusks.**

6. According to the passage, what is the **biggest difference** between **bivalves** and **univalves**?

_____

_____

_____

Hint #1:

The passage describes **both** bivalves and univalves. What is **different** about the descriptions?

Hint #2:

Can you use your word knowledge to help you answer this question? Think about the prefixes **bi-** and **uni-**. Do they give you any clue about the biggest difference between these two mollusks?

Answer: **Bivalves** have **two shells**; **univalves** have **one shell**.

The prefix **bi-** means **two**. For example, a <u>bi</u>cycle has **two** wheels.

In the same way, the prefix **uni-** means **one**, which is why a <u>uni</u>cycle has only **one** wheel.

Read the sentence below, then answer questions 7 and 8.

I only visited the Grand Canyon once, but the impression it made on me left a memory as clear as the image of my own bedroom.

7. Why does the writer **compare** the Grand Canyon to his own bedroom?

_____

_____

_____

_____

Hint #1:

How well do you know your own bedroom? Unless you just moved or have a habit of sleeping in the bathtub, you should know it pretty well!

Hint #2:

How does the author feel about the Grand Canyon?

Answer: The writer compares the Grand Canyon with his bedroom to **show how amazing the Grand Canyon was to visit and how it left a lasting impression in his memory.** He only visited it once, but he remembers it as well as his bedroom, which he knows very well.

8. From what **point of view** is the sentence from the previous page written?

(A) First person

(B) Second person

(C) Third person

(D) Not enough information to say

Hint #1:

The writer uses the word *I*. What point of view does that word suggest?

Hint #2:

This is a personal way of writing, like in a diary or a letter.

© Kaplan Publishing, Inc.

Answer: Choice **A** is correct.

The sentence above is written in **first person**. The first person is the **I** form. **Second person** is **you**, and **third person** is **he** or **she**.

Read the passage below and then answer questions 9 and 10.

There should be more bicycle lanes in our city. Many city residents ride bicycles, and they don't have enough room on the streets. Riding bicycles is healthy, good for the environment, and fun. People in our city should be encouraged to ride bicycles, and having more bicycle lanes is a good way to do that. We should also install more bicycle racks, and the bus should be cheaper to ride. The city should also provide bicycles for rent to tourists or residents.

9. Which of the following statements **least** fits in the passage?

Ⓐ "having more bicycle lanes is a good way to do that"

Ⓑ "we should also install more bicycle racks"

Ⓒ "the bus should be cheaper to ride"

Ⓓ "the city should also provide bicycles for rent"

Hint #1:

This passage is mostly about making it easier for people to ride bicycles.

Hint #2:

It's easy to connect other things that are good for the environment with bicycle riding, but this passage is mainly about bicycles.

Answer: Choice **C** is correct.

"The bus should be cheaper to ride" is the only statement that isn't about bicycles. All the other answer choices relate to the main point of the passage, which is to encourage people to ride bicycles.

10. Where would you most likely find a passage like the one on page 41 published?

Ⓐ in a phone book

Ⓑ in a cooking magazine

Ⓒ in a comic book

Ⓓ in a newspaper

Hint #1:

This author is trying to **convince people to do something**. Where do people usually publish articles trying to inform or change people's minds?

Hint #2:

The author of this passage believes that bicycles are very **important**. Where do people publish letters or articles about various important issues?

Answer: Choice **D** is correct.

You would most likely find a passage like this one published **in a newspaper**, most likely as a **letter to the editor**. This is where you usually find letters trying to inform the public or change people's minds about various important issues.

11. Which of the following statements is an **opinion**?

(A) FIFA organizes the World Cup soccer tournament, held every four years.

(B) Each World Cup is held in a different country, like the Olympics.

(C) The World Cup is the most exciting sports event.

(D) It's a tradition that World Cup players swap jerseys after each match.

Hint #1:

A **fact** is something that is always true and can be proven with tools like a dictionary or encyclopedia.

Hint #2:

An **opinion** is true only to certain people. It's a personal belief, like which flavor of ice cream you like best.

Answer: Choice **C** is an opinion.

The words "**most exciting**" tell you that choice **C** is an opinion. **Not everyone** thinks that the World Cup is the most exciting sports event. Some people like other sports, such as basketball or baseball, better than soccer. Because **you can't prove** that soccer is the most exciting sports event, it's an opinion to say that it is.

Read the passage below, then answer questions 12–16.

The art of soup making is more easily mastered than at first appears. The young housekeeper is startled at the amazingly large number of ingredients the recipe calls for, and often is discouraged. One may, with but little expense, keep at hand what is essential for the making of a good soup. Winter vegetables—turnips, carrots, celery, and onions—may be bought in large or small quantities. . . . Sweet herbs, including thyme, savory, and marjoram, are dried and put up in packages, retailing from five to ten cents. . . . Spices, including whole cloves, allspice berries, peppercorns, and stick cinnamon, should be kept on hand. These seasonings, with the addition of salt, pepper, and parsley, are the essential flavorings for stock soups.

–from: *The Boston Cooking-School Cook Book*,
  by Fannie Merritt Farmer (1918)

12. Why does the writer list the ingredients that are needed to make soup?

_____

_____

_____

Hint #1:

How does the writer describe the ingredients? Does she make them seem strange or normal?

Hint #2:

The ingredients are examples of something. What could that be?

Answer: The writer lists the ingredients that are needed to make soup **to show that making soup is easier than one might expect**. She is explaining that the ingredients needed are not hard or expensive to buy.

13. What is the **main idea** of this passage?

Ⓐ A lot of ingredients are needed to make soup.

Ⓑ Beginner cooks shouldn't try to make soup.

Ⓒ Soup is easier to make than most people think.

Ⓓ Every cook should have spices in the kitchen.

Hint #1:

This passage was written a long time ago, so the language might sound a little funny to your ears. Try not to get stuck in the words; just think about what the passage means.

Hint #2:

In this passage, a "**young housekeeper**" is a woman who has just gotten married and is learning how to run her home. At the time this book was written, most women worked at home.

Answer: Choice **C** is correct.

The main idea of this passage is that **soup is easier to make than most people think**. The introduction to the passage is a good indication of what it mainly is about.

14. What is the author's **purpose** for writing this passage?

- Ⓐ to increase sales of dried herbs and spices
- Ⓑ to discourage young cooks from making soup
- Ⓒ to discover a new way of growing turnips
- Ⓓ to teach people how to make a common meal

Hint #1:

If you're trying to figure out why a passage was written, looking at the source can help.

Hint #2:

This passage comes from the *Boston Cooking-School Cook Book*. Why do you think that book was probably written?

© Kaplan Publishing, Inc.

Answer: Choice **D** is correct.

This is from a cookbook that was written to teach people how to cook. The book tells people where to find the ingredients they need to make recipes. This purpose of this passage is **to teach people how to make a common meal**.

15. Which of the following sentences from the passage is an example of an **opinion**?

(A) The art of soup making is more easily mastered than at first appears.

(B) One may, with but little expense, keep at hand what is essential for the making of a good soup.

(C) Winter vegetables—turnips, carrots, celery, and onions— may be bought in large or small quantities

(D) These seasonings, with the addition of salt, pepper, and parsley, are the essential flavorings for stock soups.

Hint #1:

Remember, you can't prove an **opinion**, but you can prove a **fact.**

Hint #2:

Look carefully at each answer choice. Eliminate the ones that can be argued against.

Answer: Choice **A** is an opinion.

Choice A is the only statement that **can't be proven**. Some cooks might not find soups hard to make at all, while others might never get good at making them.

16. Which of the following would you expect to follow this passage?

(A) reports from other people who have made soup

(B) information about making salads and desserts

(C) a recipe for making a soup with the ingredients mentioned

(D) a note from the author saying that making soup is too difficult for most cooks

Hint #1:

This passage comes from a cookbook. What do you usually find in cookbooks?

Hint #2:

A cookbook has lots of information in it, but you're looking for what would probably come **right after** this passage, not much later in the book.

Answer: Choice **C** is correct.

This is a cookbook, so it will contain recipes. This passage talks about how easy it is to make soup, so the next thing you'd expect to see is **a recipe for making soup with the ingredients mentioned**.

Read the passage below, then answer questions 17 and 18.

David lost his backpack. He knew he had it with him when he went to the library, but he didn't have it when he got home. He went back to the library right away and saw another boy carrying the same kind of backpack as his, but in blue instead of red. David ran up to the boy and said, "Hey, you stole my backpack and painted it!"

17. Does David have enough **evidence** to come to the conclusion that he did? Why or why not?

_____

_____

_____

© Kaplan Publishing, Inc.

Hint #1:

A library is a **public place**. There are usually lots of people at the library doing homework and borrowing books for fun.

Hint #2:

Have you ever tried to paint a backpack? Do you think it is easy to do?

Answer: No. David did not have enough evidence to come to the conclusion that he did. His backpack could have still been in the library, or someone else could have taken it. That boy probably just owned the backpack in a different color.

18. What piece of information would make David's conclusion **more realistic?**

Ⓐ There were lots of other kids at the library that day.

Ⓑ The boy David saw was holding a can of red spray paint.

Ⓒ David had never lost his backpack before.

Ⓓ David lived very close to the library.

Hint #1:

The new information should make it **more likely** that the other boy has David's backpack. If it's about anything else, it won't help his conclusion make more sense.

Hint #2:

Right now, David sounds a little ridiculous. The new information should make him sound **less** ridiculous.

© Kaplan Publishing, Inc.

Answer: Choice **B** is correct.

If the boy David saw was holding a can of red spray paint, then he could have painted David's backpack red. None of the other choices has anything to do with the boy whom David is accusing, nor do they make David's story more credible.

19. Which sentence is an example of the **second-person** point of view?

(A) I watched the ants marching in a line to their anthill, like a little parade.

(B) Angela couldn't wait to get to the beach and cool off.

(C) Ravi thought the game was exciting, but Simon thought it was boring.

(D) You and Ali would probably like each other, because you both like scary movies.

Hint #1:

The **second person** is the voice you use when you talk to another person.

Hint #2:

Eliminate the answer choices that don't sound like talking to another person.

Answer: Choice **D** is correct.

"You and Ali would probably like each other, because you both like scary movies" is an example of the second-person point of view. The second person uses the word *you* and sounds the way people do in regular conversation.

You're doing a great job so far!
Are you ready for a Challenge Activity?

Good luck!

Read the following passage and then answer the questions that follow.

In both Canada and the United States the theory and indeed the practice of preserving wild life on protected areas of land have made astonishing headway since the closing years of the nineteenth century. These protected areas, some of very large size, come in two classes. First, there are those which are public property, where the protection is given by the State. Secondly, there are those where the ownership and the protection are private.

By far the most important, of course, are the public preserves. These, just by existing, show the extent to which democratic government can justify itself.

–adapted from Theodore Roosevelt's
A Book-Lover's Holidays in the Open (1916)

a) What **two types** of protected areas does Roosevelt mention?

_____

_____

_____

b) What is another way to say "**the closing years of the nineteenth century**"?

_____

c) What is the **main idea** of this passage?

Ⓐ Wildlife preservation has improved over the years.

Ⓑ Canada is better at wildlife preservation than the United States.

Ⓒ Protecting wildlife is an essential role of government.

Ⓓ Government needs to protect wildlife to prove that we need government.

Hint #1:

Roosevelt says there are two kinds of preserves. Which one does he see as better?

Hint #2:

We are now in the early 21st century. What would be another way of saying that?

Answers to Challenge Activity:

a) The two types of protected areas that Roosevelt mentions are **places protected by the state and places protected by private people**.

b) There are many possible variations of this phrase. One other way to say. "the closing years of the nineteenth century" is "**the end of the 1800s**."

c) Choice **C** is correct.
The main idea of this passage is that **protecting wildlife is an essential role of government**.

Let's take a quick test and see how much you've learned during this climb up *SCORE!* Mountain.

Good luck!

Read the passage below and then answer questions 1–3.

Consideration for the rights and feelings of others is not merely a rule for behavior in public but the very foundation upon which social life is built.

Rule of etiquette the first . . . is:

Never do anything that is unpleasant to others.

Never take more than your share—whether of the road in driving a car, of chairs on a boat or seats on a train, or food at the table.

People who picnic along the public highway leaving a clutter of greasy paper and swill (not a pretty name, but neither is it a pretty object!) for other people to walk or drive past, and to make a breeding place for flies, and furnish nourishment for rats, choose a disgusting way to repay the land-owner for the liberty they took in temporarily occupying his property.

–from Emily Post's *Etiquette, Chapter 5:*
On the Street and in Public

1. What is the author's purpose for writing this passage?

(A) to instruct the public in proper behavior

(B) to educate children about how to stage a proper picnic

(C) to complain about the actions of an acquaintance

(D) to provide examples of sharing for a math problem

2. Read the following sentence from the passage:

Consideration for the rights and feelings of others is not merely a rule for behavior in public but the very foundation upon which social life is built.

What does the author most likely mean by this sentence?

Ⓐ Politeness is important in all areas of life.

Ⓑ You can be more relaxed at home than in public.

Ⓒ Social situations are times for sharing.

Ⓓ Consideration is an outdated way of relating to people.

3. From what point of view is this passage written?

_____

_____

Read the passage below, then answer questions 4 and 5.

Welcome to the Tastie Restaurant family of employees! We're glad to have you on the team. Remember to follow the instructions below every time you arrive for work so that your shift is safe and successful.

1. Arrive 15 minutes before your shift begins.
2. Change into your Tastie uniform in the appropriate (male/female) changing area.
3. Place your belongings in a locker and lock it securely with your own lock.
4. Tie long hair back in a ponytail, braid, or bun.
5. Put on a hat.
6. Wash your hands.
7. Punch in on the time clock to start payment for your shift.
8. Proceed to your station.

4. What is one possible complaint that Tastie workers might reasonably have about the order of steps above?

Ⓐ They should be able to place their belongings in a locker before changing into their uniform.

Ⓑ They should be able to proceed to their stations before changing into their uniforms.

Ⓒ They should not have to wash their hands before proceeding to their stations.

Ⓓ They should be able to punch in before they change into their uniforms.

5. The staff is planning to add more information to Step 5 to make the health regulations clearer. Which of the following would be the best addition to "Put on a hat . . ."?

Ⓐ . . . that expresses your personality.

Ⓑ . . . of your favorite school or town team.

Ⓒ . . . that covers all of your hair.

Ⓓ . . . to keep you warm during your shift.

Answers to test questions:

1. Choice **A** is correct.
Emily Post wrote this passage on etiquette **to instruct the public in proper behavior**.

2. Choice **A** is correct.
In the sentence, the author writes that the rights and feelings of others are "the very foundation upon which social life is built." She is clearly trying to stress the fact that **politeness is important in all areas of life**.

3. This passage is written from a **second person point of view**. It is written in second person because instructions are being given directly to **you**, the reader.

4. Choice **D** is correct.
One possible complaint that Tastie workers might reasonably have about the order of steps is that **they should be able to punch in before they change into their uniforms**.
It can be argued that they should be paid beginning when they arrive at work and not lose the time it takes to get changed. Also, they wouldn't want to be considered late if they arrive on time and need to get changed before they could punch in.

5. Choice **C** is correct.
Revising Step 5 to read "**Put on a hat that covers all of your hair**" makes it clearer that keeping your hair covered when handling food is a necessary health regulation.

Celebrate!

Let's take a fun break before we go to the next base camp. You've earned it!

Let's get up and get active!

Get yourself moving during this study break!

Try shooting a basketball into a basket and set a goal to make a certain number of shots. See if you can reach your goal!

You can also challenge a friend or relative to do the same and see who makes the most shots!

Congratulations!
You're getting closer to the top of *SCORE!* Mountain.

If a basketball hoop is not available, try kicking a ball into a net.

Or take some time to participate in some other sport or exercise—whatever is your favorite!

Whatever activity you choose, you are refreshing your body and mind, which is always a great idea!

Good luck and have fun!
You deserve it for working so hard!

Read the passage below, then answer questions 1 and 2 on the following page.

The Fox and the Goat

By an unlucky chance a Fox fell into a deep well from which he could not get out. A Goat passed by shortly afterwards, and asked the Fox what he was doing down there. "Oh, have you not heard?" said the Fox; "there is going to be a great drought, so I jumped down here in order to be sure to have water by me. Why don't you come down too?" The Goat thought well of this advice, and jumped down into the well. But the Fox immediately jumped on her back, and by putting his foot on her long horns managed to jump up to the edge of the well. "Good-bye, friend," said the Fox, "remember next time, NEVER TRUST THE ADVICE OF A MAN IN DIFFICULTIES."

–from *The Harvard Classics*, by Aesop

1. This passage is an example of

    (A) a biography.

    (B) a fable.

    (C) a short story.

    (D) a monologue.

Hint #1:

The **main characters** in this passage are **animals**. What kind of story often uses animals as the main characters?

Hint #2:

This passage was written by Aesop. Have you ever heard of Aesop before? What kind of stories did he write?

Answer: Choice **B** is correct.

This passage is an example of **a fable**. Fables are generally about **animals**, and they always include a lesson at the end. **Aesop** was the most famous fable writer in history.

2. The last line of the passage is an example of a

(A) moral.

(B) metaphor.

(C) punch line.

(D) theme.

Hint #1:

How does the last line relate to the rest of the passage?

Hint #2:

This is the kind of story that you might tell a small child to teach the child a lesson about life.

Answer: Choice **A** is correct.

The last line of the passage is an example of a **moral**, or lesson of the story. It sums up the action in the story and tells you what you should have learned from it.

Read the passage below, then answer questions 3 and 4.

Claude rose and dressed, a simple operation which took very little time. He crept down two flights of stairs, feeling his way in the dusk, his red hair standing up in peaks, like a cock's comb. He went through the kitchen into the adjoining washroom, which held two porcelain stands with running water. Everybody had washed before going to bed, apparently, and the bowls were ringed with a dark sediment which the hard, alkaline water had not dissolved. Shutting the door on this disorder, he turned back to the kitchen, took Mahailey's tin basin, doused his face and head in cold water, and began to plaster down his wet hair.

–from *One of Ours*, by Willa Cather

3. Which of the following is an example of **simile**?

Ⓐ "a simple operation which took very little time"

Ⓑ "his red hair standing up in peaks, like a cock's comb"

Ⓒ "everybody had washed before going to bed, apparently"

Ⓓ "shutting the door on this disorder, he turned back to the kitchen"

Hint #1:

Similes compare two things using the words **like** or **as**.

Hint #2:

What quality do all similes share?

Answer: Choice **B** is correct.

The phrase **"his red hair standing up in peaks, like a cock's comb"** compares Claude's red hair to a cock's comb, using the word **like**.

© Kaplan Publishing, Inc.

4. What does the **setting** tell you about the family?

(A) They are successful in business.

(B) They take great care with their belongings.

(C) They do not have much money.

(D) They don't like Claude's hair to stand up.

Hint #1:

Does this seem like a **happy** place to live? Would you want to live in that house?

Hint #2:

An **image** is a description that creates a picture in your head. What images let you know the setting of the story? Read them carefully and see what they make you think.

Answer: Choice **C** is correct.

The setting tells you that **they do not have much money**. Claude gets up very early in the morning. He wears simple clothes. The water is hard and unpleasant. The whole family used two bowls to wash. All the descriptions of the setting suggest that this is a rough life and this family does not have much money.

Here is the opening of Willa Cather's *One of Ours*, which comes before the passage you just read.

Read it, then answer question 5.

Claude Wheeler opened his eyes before the sun was up and vigorously shook his younger brother, who lay in the other half of the same bed.

"Ralph, Ralph, get awake! Come down and help me wash the car."

"What for?"

"Why, aren't we going to the circus today?"

"Car's all right. Let me alone." The boy turned over and pulled the sheet up to his face, to shut out the light which was beginning to come through the curtainless windows.

5. How does the information in this story opening change the tone of the story?

(A) The circus sounds more fun than it did before.

(B) Claude is less sympathetic than he seemed.

(C) The family doesn't seem to get along very well.

(D) The situation is happier than it first appeared.

Hint #1:

Now we know that Claude **doesn't have to** get up this early every day. Does that make things seem better or worse for him?

Hint #2:

Why does he have to get up early in the story?

Answer: Choice **D** is correct.

The information in this story opening shows that **the situation is happier than it first appeared**. Claude is getting up early to get the car ready to go to the circus with his brother. It seems as though they are having a special experience, which is why he needs to be up so early in the day. The story seems happier once you know the opening.

Here is the next section of the story from Willa Cather's
One of Ours.

Read it, then answer question 6.

Old Mahailey herself came in from the yard, with her apron full of corn-cobs to start a fire in the kitchen stove. She smiled at him in the foolish fond way she often had with him when they were alone.

"What air you gittin' up for a-ready, boy? You goin' to the circus before breakfast? Don't you make no noise, else you'll have 'em all down here before I git my fire a-goin'."

6. How does the entrance of Old Mahailey **change** how you see Claude?

_____

_____

_____

Hint #1:

What does Old Mahailey think of Claude? That "**foolish fond way**" she looks at him should tell you.

Hint #2:

Does Old Mahailey say anything that makes you think about why Claude is up so early in the morning?

Answer: Claude seems more like an enthusiastic boy than like a hard-working young man. He's up early because he's excited to go to the circus. Old Mahailey thinks he's funny, teasing him for "goin' to the circus before breakfast."

© Kaplan Publishing, Inc.

Here's the next passage of the story from Willa Cather's
One of Ours.

Read it, then answer questions 7–10.

"All right, Mahailey." Claude caught up his cap and ran out of doors, down the hillside toward the barn. The sun popped up over the edge of the prairie like a broad, smiling face; the light poured across the close-cropped August pastures and the hilly, timbered windings of Lovely Creek,—a clear little stream with a sand bottom, that curled and twisted playfully about through the south section of the big Wheeler ranch. It was a fine day to go to the circus at Frankfort, a fine day to do anything; the sort of day that must, somehow, turn out well.

7. How does the **new setting information** change your thoughts about the story?

_____

_____

_____

Hint #1:

Did you expect that the Wheelers lived on a "**big . . . ranch**"? Given what we saw in the first section, probably not.

Hint #2:

How does the description of the sun rising change the feeling of the story?

Answer: The imagery in this section is very happy and excited, and probably makes you feel more positive about the Wheeler family. The sun rises like a "**smiling face**," the creek is named "**Lovely**," and the whole day now sounds wonderful. With this new information, we see that the Wheelers are a happy, secure family. They probably just lived long ago, when modern conveniences weren't common.

8. What image does the description of the creek suggest?

(A) an angry bull charging at the color red

(B) a kitten winding around its owner's legs

(C) a snake slithering toward its prey

(D) a fish floating along aimlessly

Hint #1:

The author uses the words *curled* and *twisted playfully* to describe the creek. Which of the choices above sounds like it would fit with those words?

Hint #2:

Cross out the answer choices that don't seem to fit the **image** of the creek in your head.

Answer: Choice **B** is correct.

The image created by the description of the creek suggests **a kitten winding around its owner's legs**. The creek is described as a happy and lively character. The description makes it sound innocent and curious. The only choice that matches all of these ideas is choice B, which is about a kitten.

9. From what you have read of the story so far, what is the tone?

(A) disappointed

(B) eager

(C) tired

(D) angry

Hint #1:

The **tone** is the **overall feeling** of the story.

Hint #2:

When you think about the tone, consider **all the pieces of the passage together**.

Answer: Choice **B** is correct.

The tone of the story is **eager**. Claude is very excited to go to the circus. He wakes up extra early, wants to get the necessary work done right away, and is teased by Old Mahailey. He watches the sun rise and feels happy and thrilled about the day to come.

Read the passage below, then answer questions 10 and 11.

I'm nobody! Who are you?
Are you nobody, too?
Then there's a pair of us—don't tell!
They'd banish us, you know.

How dreary to be somebody!
How public, like a frog

To tell your name the livelong day
To an admiring bog!

–from *Complete Poems*, by Emily Dickinson

10. What is the **main idea** of this poem?

_____

_____

_____

_____

Hint #1:

It's **not** about a frog.

Hint #2:

Dickinson doesn't like that being "**somebody**" is so "**public**." What types of people have "public lives"?

Answer: This poem is about being famous and how it doesn't sound very appealing to the writer. She uses the image of the frog because frogs are noisy animals, croaking all day in the bogs where they live.

11. What effect does the **punctuation** have in this poem?

    Ⓐ It makes the poem read very evenly.

    Ⓑ It tells the reader that the writer is worried about something.

    Ⓒ It produces a youthful feeling.

    Ⓓ It is silly and makes the poem feel unreliable.

Hint #1:

Exclamation points can mean many different things. What do you think they mean here?

Hint #2:

Imagine the writer talking. How would she sound when she said this poem?

Answer: Choice **C** is correct.

Emily Dickinson frequently used punctuation to emphasize words or phrases in her poems. She seems to be having fun in this poem and isn't really worried, giving her work a **youthful feeling**.

Read the passage below, then answer questions 12 and 13.

Brandon loved the last day of school. Every year, he tore off as the last bell rang, making a beeline for his favorite ice cream store. He put both hands on the counter, stood up on the tops of his toes, and said to the scooper, "I'll have a Rocky Road cone, because this is the end of the road!" The scooper laughed, Brandon laughed, and he'd end up with an extra scoop for free.

12. Why does Brandon order Rocky Road ice cream?

Ⓐ the ice cream store is on a rocky road

Ⓑ the ice cream store is at the end of a road

Ⓒ it is a symbol for the end of the school year

Ⓓ he gets an extra scoop when he orders that flavor

Hint #1:

Why does the scooper laugh when Brandon orders his ice cream? What is so funny about his order?

Hint #2:

The phrase "**the end of the road**" is an expression that means more than just what it says. Have you ever heard anyone say it? What did they mean?

Answer: Choice **C** is correct.

Brandon ordered Rocky Road ice cream **because it is a symbol for the end of the school year**. The phrase "the end of the road" means that something is over or that it can't go on any longer. Brandon orders Rocky Road because it's a symbol for ending the "**rocky road**" of the school year. That's why the scooper thinks it's funny and gives Brandon an extra scoop for free.

13. What does the author mean when he says that Brandon "tore off"?

_____

_____

_____

_____

Hint #1:

Did Brandon actually tear anything?

Hint #2:

What is Brandon doing when the author says that he "**tore off**"?

Answer: "**Tore off**" is a more creative way to say "**ran quickly**." One thing that authors do is use **figurative language**. It's a way of writing that creates images in your head and makes stories more interesting to read.

Read the following passage, then answer questions 14–16.

Every day after school, Jorge took the bus uptown and walked to his grandmother's house. She would watch him in the afternoon while his parents were at work. He always looked forward to going to her house, because she fed him lots of snacks and had a funny, talking parrot. Sometimes Jorge taught the parrot to say things. Then when his parents came to pick him up after work, the parrot would say to them, "Jorge is the best." One day, he decided to do something special. At the end of the afternoon, when his parents arrived, the parrot fluffed itself and said, "Jorge's *grandmother* is the best."

14. Why does the author include the **last two sentences** in the passage?

_____

_____

_____

_____

Hint #1:

What is **special** about what Jorge does?

Hint #2:

How does Jorge feel about his grandmother?

Answer: **The author includes the last two sentences to show what a great and strong relationship Jorge has with his grandmother.**
Jorge definitely loves his grandmother and enjoys going to her house after school. When he taught the parrot to say how great she was, he did that to show her, and his parents, how much he loved her.

15. What is the **main idea** of this passage?

    Ⓐ Parrots can be taught to say things easily.

    Ⓑ Parents should never let grandmothers watch their children.

    Ⓒ Jorge has a close, loving family.

    Ⓓ Jorge's grandmother has a parrot.

Hint #1:

Think about the story from **Jorge's point of view**. What would **he** say the main idea is?

Hint #2:

Make sure that the main idea is actually **supported** by things the author says in the passage!

Answer: Choice **C** is correct.

The main idea of this passage is that **Jorge has a close, loving family**. Jorge spends the afternoons with his grandmother and loves doing so. He also seems to like the parrot and his parents.

16. What **change** do you see in Jorge, based on the two things he taught the parrot to say?

_____

_____

_____

Hint #1:

What's the difference between the two things Jorge taught the parrot?

Hint #2:

Imagine being Jorge's parents. How would you see these two things differently?

Answer: Based on the two things he had the parrot say, **Jorge is learning that it's nice to tell people that you love them and appreciate them**. First, Jorge had the parrot talk about him, probably to be funny. Then, he had it talk about his grandmother, so he was thinking about someone other than himself. That shows that he was growing and learning that it's nice to tell people that you love them and appreciate them.

Read the following passage, then answer questions 17–19.

Shana loved to collect figurines of dogs. She would line them up on her desk and imagine that they were her pets. She didn't want to tell anyone about her imaginary pets, because she thought it was embarrassing, but she really wanted to own a pet and she didn't have one. Every afternoon, she walked past a house with an adorable, tiny white dog. The dog just sat at the front walk, seemingly waiting for Shana to come past. She would pat the dog and imagine it being hers. But every day, she had to leave the dog to its owners and walk to her home and her silent, imaginary friends.

17. What is the **tone** of this passage?

_____

_____

_____

Hint #1:

How did Shana **feel** about her dog figurines? Did they make her happy?

Hint #2:

Look at the **last sentence** of the passage. How would you feel if you were Shana?

Answer: The tone of this passage is sad and lonely.
Shana wanted to own a dog, but she didn't own one. She visited the dog at the other house, but it wasn't hers. She felt sad and wished that she had a dog of her own.

18. Why does the author include the information about Shana's dog figurines?

(A) they show her creativity

(B) they are a symbol of her unhappiness

(C) to show that Shana doesn't want to own a dog

(D) to make it more of a surprise when Shana sees the neighbor's dog

Hint #1:

The figurines are described at the beginning of the passage. Usually information at the beginning of a passage sets up the rest of the story in some way.

Hint #2:

The author says that Shana is embarrassed about her figurines. Why would she be embarrassed about her own collection?

Answer: Choice **B** is correct.

The author includes the information about Shana's dog figurines **because they are a symbol of her unhappiness**. The figurines are the closest things Shana can have to a real dog, but they aren't real dogs, so she's embarrassed about playing with them because she knows it's kind of silly. She knows she's only playing with them because she is lonely and unhappy.

19. What does the author mean by saying that the dog was "seemingly waiting for Shana to come past"?

_____

_____

_____

Hint #1:

Do you think the dog was actually waiting for Shana to come past the house?

Hint #2:

Why might Shana think that the dog was waiting for her to arrive?

Answer: The author is really saying that **Shana wanted to believe that the dog was waiting for her**.
Shana wants a dog to love, and she wants to believe that this dog wants to be hers. The dog was probably just sitting outside its house as it always does, but in Shana's wishful thinking, it was waiting for her.

Challenge Activity

You're doing a great job so far!
Are you ready for a Challenge Activity?

Good luck!

Read the following passage, then answer the questions that follow.

With hands moving all about, the schoolteacher walked up and down the classroom and talked very quickly. She talked about whatever random thought entered her head. Once she talked to her class about John Dumont and mentioned some quirky little stories concerning the life of this dead writer. The stories were told with the air of one who knew him intimately, as if he was a close friend of hers. Her students were always interested in her stories but were now somewhat confused, thinking that John Dumont must be someone who had lived in their town, in Summerville. But the truth was that he had not.

a) Why did the students think that John Dumont had lived in Summerville?

_____

_____

_____

b) What is the function of this passage?

_____

_____

_____

c) Based on the information in the passage, is she a good teacher in your opinion?

_____

_____

_____

Hint #1:

What does the teacher do and say? What kind of information does she tell them about John Dumont?

Hint #2:

The **function of the passage** is the author's reason for writing it. What is this passage mostly about?

Answers to Challenge Activity: Answers may vary slightly, but as long as your answer touches on the same points as the sample answers below, then you're on the right track!

a) **The students think that John Dumont lived in Summerville because the teacher talked about him as though he was a friend.**

b) **The function of this passage is to describe a character. This whole paragraph is about the teacher. It's part of a longer story, and you could guess that it's the part of the story in which the teacher is described to readers for the first time. The whole function of the passage is to give you an idea of who the teacher is and what she is like.**

c) This question asks for your opinion, so everyone's answer can be different!
Based on the information in the passage, it seems as though she's good at keeping the students interested, but she's a little strange. It sounds like she's making up some of what she's teaching them.

Let's take a quick test and see how much you've learned during this climb up *SCORE!* Mountain.

Good luck!

Read the passage below, then answer questions 1–3.

It is a truth universally acknowledged, that a single man in possession of a good fortune must be in want of a wife. However little known the feelings or views of such a man may be on his first entering a neighborhood, this truth is so well fixed in the minds of the surrounding families, that he is considered as the rightful property of some one or other of their daughters.

–from *Pride and Prejudice*, by Jane Austen

1. What is the tone of this passage?

Ⓐ strict

Ⓑ lighthearted

Ⓒ scientific

Ⓓ sentimental

2. What is the author's purpose for writing this passage?

(A) to explain how difficult it is for wealthy men to find wives

(B) to illustrate how much the neighborhood wants to help single men

(C) to make fun of the competition among families to have their daughters marry wealthy men

(D) to tell families that they are treating the young men and women in their neighborhoods terribly

3. As it is used in the passage, what do you think the phrase *in want of* means?

_____

_____

_____

Read the following passage, then answer questions 4 and 5.

Yes, it was right glorious out in the country. In the midst of the sunshine there lay an old farm, with deep canals about it, and from the wall down to the water grew great burdocks, so high that little children could stand upright under the loftiest of them. It was just as wild there as in the deepest wood, and here sat a Duck upon her nest; she had to hatch her ducklings; but she was almost tired out before the little ones came; and then she so seldom had visitors. The other ducks liked better to swim about in the canals than to run up to sit down under a burdock, and cackle with her.

–from *Tales*, by Hans Christian Andersen

4. What kind of passage is this?

Ⓐ a play

Ⓑ a poem

Ⓒ a fairy tale

Ⓓ a historical novel

5. What effect does the setting have on the plot?

Ⓐ It makes the story feel dangerous.

Ⓑ It makes you not care about the duck.

Ⓒ It gives a feeling of overgrowth and lack of control.

Ⓓ It makes you like the duck and wonder why no one visits.

Answers to test questions:

1. Choice **B** is correct.
    The tone of Jane Austen's passage is **lighthearted**. It playfully describes the eagerness of some families to have their daughters marry wealthy men.

2. Choice **C** is correct.
    The author's purpose for writing this passage is **to make fun of the competition among families to have their daughters marry wealthy men**.

3. As it is used in the passage, the phrase *in want of* means "**needing**" or "**wanting**."
    When Austen writes "that a single man in possession of a good fortune must be in want of a wife," she is saying that wealthy men want or need wives.

4. Choice **C** is correct.
    The passage by Hans Christian Andersen is an example of **a fairy tale**. A fairy tale is a type of story in which fantastic and improbable events occur.

5. Choice **D** is correct.
    The setting of the story **makes you like the duck and wonder why no one visits**.

Celebrate!

Let's take a fun break before we go to the next base camp. You've earned it!

Get permission from a parent or adult to take a nature walk in your local park!

There are lots of fun things to do during a nature walk:

- You can get some fresh air and enjoy all the different trees, plants, and flowers that live in the park. See how many different kinds you can find!

- Gather some leaves and start a scrapbook of all the different ones you collect!

Congratulations!
You're halfway to the top of *SCORE!* Mountain.

- Look around for different types of birds during your nature walk. If you have binoculars, then your experience can be extra fun!
- Plus, a nature walk is refreshing and a great exercise!
- If you'd like, try to convince a friend or family member to go with you and talk about all the beautiful and interesting things you discover along the way.

Good luck and have fun!

You deserve it for working so hard!

Read the information below, then answer questions 1 and 2.

Angel's teacher asked the students to conduct research about how an important building or monument was built and to write about what they learn. Angel wants to write about the Eiffel Tower in Paris.

1. To complete this assignment, Angel will write a

(A) poem.

(B) factual report.

(C) book report.

(D) letter to the editor.

Hint #1:

What **subject** do you think Angel's teacher teaches?

Hint #2:

Angel's **assignment** is to write about information he learns from many nonfiction books.

Answer: Choice **B** is correct.

To complete this assignment, Angel will write a **factual report**.

Angel's assignment is to write a report based on **research of facts**. His report will be based on many books, not just one, and it will be about what he learns, not about what he thought of the books. He probably got this assignment in his social studies class.

© Kaplan Publishing, Inc.

2. What would be the **best source** for Angel to use to research his report?

(A) architecture magazines

(B) French adventure stories

(C) the Eiffel Tower Web site

(D) a play about Gustave Eiffel

Hint #1:

Angel's report needs to be based on **facts**. Which one of these sources will give him facts?

Hint #2:

The **best** source is the one that will give him the **most** information about the Eiffel Tower.

Answer: Choice **C** is correct.

The best source for Angel to use to research his report is **the Eiffel Tower Web site**. Angel needs to find facts about how the Eiffel Tower was built, which its Web site is sure to have.

Here is part of Angel's report. It may contain some errors.
Read it, then answer questions 3–7.

(1) In 2005, over 6 million people visited the Eiffel Tower. (2) It took over two years to build. (3) And was built to celebrate the 100th anniversary of the French Revolution. (4) It took 271 workers to do all the work to build it. (5) The Eiffel Tower designers used skills they learned building bridges to make the tower stand so tall. (6) The tower was constructed in 18,000 small pieces. (7) Those pieces be held together by 2,500,000 rivets. (8) The builders used lots of amazing ways of building to get the work done. (9) They even made special airtight boxes that they filled with air so they could work underwater on the foundation.

3. Which sentence below would be **best to** add to the beginning of Angel's report?

Ⓐ The Eiffel Tower is one of the most famous structures in Paris.

Ⓑ The Eiffel Tower is really a beautiful structure.

Ⓒ I don't really like how the Eiffel Tower looks.

Ⓓ Gustave Eiffel was given a Legion of Honor medal for his work.

Hint #1:

The **first sentence** has an important job: it **introduces** the topic!

Hint #2:

Remember, this is a **research report**. Angel shouldn't give his opinion, only the **facts**.

Answer: Choice **A** is correct.

The new first sentence should introduce the topic, which is the Eiffel Tower. **The Eiffel Tower is one of the most famous structures in Paris**, and saying that is a good way to start the report. It tells readers what the report will be about.

4. What should Angel do with **sentence (1)** to make the essay read better?

(A) Leave it where it is.

(B) Move it to after sentence (2).

(C) Move it to after sentence (5).

(D) Remove it.

Hint #1:

Sentence (1) is about the Eiffel Tower today.

Hint #2:

Try each answer choice. Which one makes the essay read better?

Answer: Choice **D** is correct.

This paragraph is about how the Eiffel Tower was **built**. Sentence (1) is about people visiting the Eiffel Tower. It isn't connected to the rest of the paragraph, which is about how it was made. The best thing for Angel to do is **remove sentence (1)**.

© Kaplan Publishing, Inc.

5. Which is **not** a complete sentence?

Ⓐ sentence (3)

Ⓑ sentence (4)

Ⓒ sentence (5)

Ⓓ sentence (6)

Hint #1:

A full sentence needs to have a **subject** and a **verb**.

Hint #2:

A complete sentence makes sense alone, without the sentence before or after it.

Answer: Choice **A** is correct.

Sentence (3) is **not** a complete sentence, because it doesn't have a **subject**. What was built to celebrate the 100th anniversary of the French Revolution? You have to read the sentence before it to know what this sentence is really about.

© Kaplan Publishing, Inc.

6. What **title** could Angel give his report?

_____

_____

_____

_____

Hint #1:

What is the report **mostly** about? Make sure that's in the title!

Hint #2:

The title should be the **most general thing** the report is about.

Answer: Your title may be slightly different but should be something like "**How the Eiffel Tower Was Built**." If your title is similar, then it's probably a good one. If your title doesn't talk about the Eiffel Tower or how it was built, then it might need some more work.

7. Read **sentence (7)** again:

<u>Those pieces be held together</u> by 2,500,000 rivets.

What is the **correct way** to write the underlined portion of **sentence (7)**?

(A) Those pieces be held together

(B) Those pieces is held together

(C) Those pieces are held together

(D) Those pieces will be held together

Hint #1:

Is the subject word **singular** or **plural**? Make sure the verb matches it!

Hint #2:

The pieces were put together a long time ago, but they're still connected **now** (or the Eiffel Tower would have fallen down!). Make sure the verb **fits** that idea.

Answer: Choice **C** is correct.

"Those pieces" is a **plural subject**, so the verb must be plural, too. Also, the pieces were connected a long time ago, so the answer can't be in the future. The best match is *are*, because it's plural and it fits the idea that the pieces were connected a long time ago and are still connected now.

© Kaplan Publishing, Inc.

Read the following passage, then answer questions 8 and 9.

Hailey saw a photograph of Mia Hamm and wondered what it would be like to be a famous soccer player like her. For her next creative writing assignment, she will write about what she thinks Mia Hamm's life is like.

8. To complete this assignment, Hailey will write a

Ⓐ research report.

Ⓑ biography.

Ⓒ personal letter.

Ⓓ short story.

Hint #1:

When you read the passage, look for clues as to what type of writing assignment this will be.

Hint #2:

Remember, this assignment is for a **creative writing class**.

Answer: Choice **D** is the correct answer.
To complete this assignment, Hailey will write a **short story**.
Even though Mia Hamm is a real person, Hailey isn't writing about her actual life. Instead, she is using her **imagination** to write a story about what she thinks it would be like to be Mia Hamm.

9. If Hailey wants to obtain information from the Mia Hamm Foundation, she should write a

(A) letter of complaint.

(B) personal letter.

(C) letter of request.

(D) letter to the editor.

Hint #1:

Remember, this letter is for a **school project**.

Hint #2:

Hailey's goal is to get **information**. Which one of these letters sounds like it would best help her get information?

Answer: Choice **C** is correct.

Haley should write a **letter of request**. Hailey wants to get information. Therefore, her letter needs to ask for information for her project. **Request** is another word for **ask**.

Read the passage below, then answer questions 10–12.

We at the *Daily Trumpet* support Marco Marconi for class president. He wants the same things we want: better choices in the cafeteria, longer recess at lunchtime, and new computers in the library. He cares about our school and wants to make it better. He is honest, and he is always working hard. So what if he hasn't been president before? Isn't it time for a change? His dad makes really good chocolate chip cookies. So join us in voting for Marco on November 4!

10. Where would you expect to see this passage?

Ⓐ a school newspaper

Ⓑ a magazine

Ⓒ a book of poetry

Ⓓ a travel brochure

Hint #1:

What do you think the *Daily Trumpet* is?

Hint #2:

Where do you think you would find stories about whom to vote for in an election?

Answer: Choice **A** is correct.

You would expect to find stories about whom to vote for in a class election in the editorials and opinions section of a **school newspaper**.

11. Which sentence from the passage should be removed?

(A) We at the *Daily Trumpet* support Marco Marconi for class president.

(B) He cares about our school and wants to make it better.

(C) Isn't it time for a change?

(D) His dad makes really good chocolate chip cookies.

Hint #1:

You should only remove a sentence that doesn't make sense or fit in with the rest of the passage.

Hint #2:

Is one of the answer choices not really on the topic of voting for Marco for class president? If so, that's a good choice to remove.

Answer: Choice **D** should be removed.

It's nice to know that **Marco's dad makes really good chocolate chip cookies**, but it doesn't have anything to do with the election. This passage is about why Marco is a good candidate for class president. The information about his dad doesn't belong here.

12. Which answer choice below shows the **best** way to write the following sentence?

He is honest, and he is always working hard.

(A) He is honest and working.

(B) He is honest and hardworking.

(C) He is honest and always working.

(D) He is honest, and is he working always hard.

Hint #1:

Sometimes, the **simplest** and **most straightforward** version is the best.

Hint #2:

Make sure that you don't change the meaning of the sentence!

Answer: Choice **B** is a better way to say the sentence.

You don't need to say "he is" twice in a row. The phrase "is always working hard" really just means "hardworking." The best version of the sentence, **"He is honest and hardworking,"** gets that idea across in the fewest words and most straightforward way.

13. **Combine** the two sentences below into one.

Our town has some wonderful museums. The prices to visit them are too high.

Hint #1:

Do both the sentences give you the same feeling about the museums?

Hint #2:

When you connect two sentences, you usually need a **connecting word**, such as **and**, **but**, or **so**.

Answer: Our town has some wonderful museums, but the prices to visit them are too high.

The **first sentence** says something **positive** about museums. The **second sentence** says something **negative** about museums. The best way to connect two sentences that say two different things about the same issue is with the word **but**. You also need a **comma** to connect the two parts in the new sentence.

Read the following passage, then answer questions 14–17.

Dear Drew,

    Welcome to our family! I know you were just born <u>yesterday, I</u> already feel as if you'll be a really good brother. I can't wait until you are big enough to play with Lily and me. We have a lot of fun. We play on the computer and we do gymnastics and we go to the beach when it's nice out. When will you start to talk? I'm going to help my Mommy take care of you I'm a good helper. I even help Lily clean up when she makes a mess. Lily is really messy.

See you on Tuesday when you get to come home!

Love,
Maya

14. Maya should change the **underlined portion** to read

  Ⓐ "yesterday, so I".

  Ⓑ "yesterday, and I".

  Ⓒ "yesterday, but I".

  Ⓓ "yesterday I".

Hint #1:

Drew was born yesterday. Do you expect Maya to know if he will be a good brother?

Hint #2:

What word should you use if the second half of the sentence is surprising, given the first half?

Answer: Choice **C** is correct.

Maya should change the sentence with the underlined portion to read: **I know you were just born yesterday, *but* I already feel as if you'll be a really good brother**. Drew was born yesterday, so no one knows him very well yet. However, Maya still thinks he will be a good brother. That means the second half of the sentence is a bit of a surprise. The connecting word that shows that change is *but*.

15. How can Maya **edit** this sentence to make it **easier to read**?

> We play on the computer and we do gymnastics and we go to the beach when it's nice out.

(A) We play on the computer and we do gymnastics and go to the beach when it's nice out.

(B) We play on the computer, do gymnastics, and go to the beach when it's nice out.

(C) We play on the computer. We do gymnastics. We go to the beach when it's nice out.

(D) We play on the computer and we go to the beach when it's nice out.

Hint #1:

Make sure Maya doesn't leave out any of their fun activities!

Hint #2:

The three things Maya mentions feel like a group. What's the best way to list items in a group?

Answer: Choice **B** is correct.

Maya can make these three things into a **list**, using **commas** to separate the items. She doesn't need to say *we* before each item on the list. The best way to write the sentence would be: **We play on the computer, do gymnastics, and go to the beach when it's nice out.**

16. How can Maya **divide** the sentence below into two sentences?

> I'm going to help my Mommy take care of you I'm a good helper.

_____

_____

_____

Hint #1:

To divide a sentence into two sentences, you need to **add punctuation** somewhere.

Hint #2:

Each of the new sentences needs a **subject** and a **verb**.

Answer: The two sentences should read: **I'm going to help my Mommy take care of you. I'm a good helper**.

Each of these two sentences is complete; they each have correct punctuation as well as a subject and a verb.

17. Why is it surprising that Maya wrote this letter to Drew?

(A) she doesn't even know if she likes him yet

(B) she doesn't know how to read and write

(C) he hasn't come home yet

(D) Drew can't understand it

Hint #1:

Look carefully for clues in the reading passage.

Hint #2:

Make sure that you **don't guess** anything about Maya or Drew that isn't supported by the passage.

Answer: Choice **D** is correct.

It's surprising that Maya wrote this letter to Drew **because Drew can't understand it**. Drew was born yesterday, so he's a newborn baby. He can't understand anything yet, so it's funny that Maya wrote a letter to him.

Obviously she can read and write, because she wrote the letter. She says that she already likes him. She writes the letter to welcome him before he gets home from the hospital.

18. Kashmira just went on a trip with her family. She wants to write something special to describe the mountains she saw and how beautiful they were to her. Kashmira could write a

(A) poem.

(B) research report.

(C) business letter.

(D) scientific article.

Hint #1:

Which choice would be a personal way of writing?

Hint #2:

Which one of these would you use to describe something beautiful?

Answer: Choice **A** is correct.

Kashmira could write a **poem** to describe the mountains.

Writing a poem is a good way to express your personal feelings about something you find very beautiful.

19. Kashmira's teacher likes what she wrote and suggests that Kashmira learn more about **someone who lives** in the mountains she visited. Then Kashmira can write a

(A) play.

(B) newspaper article.

(C) biography.

(D) book review.

Hint #1:

Kashmira will write specifically about someone who lives in the mountains she visited. Which one of these types of writing is about **people**?

Hint #2:

Kashmira will be writing something after learning new information. Which of these types of writing uses **research** on a particular person?

Answer: Choice **C** is correct.

If Kashmira wants to write about someone who lives in the mountains she visited, she can write a **biography**. A biography is an account of somebody's life.

You're doing a great job so far!
Are you ready for a Challenge Activity?

Good luck!

Read the sentences below, which are part of a passage that is out of order, then answer the questions that follow.

(1) If a spider plant doesn't have enough room for its roots to grow, it will send out a shoot. (2) Spider plants are an amazing example of nature's intelligence. (3) These "babies" can take root nearby and start their own plants. (4) Once the "babies" have rooted, the shoot connecting them to the original plant disappears. (5) They have figured out a way to grow even if they don't have enough space for their roots to expand. (6) The shoot will then produce several "baby" plants that look like the legs on a spider, which is how the plant got its name. (7) Spiders have eight legs.

a) Which sentence should the writer remove from the passage?

Ⓐ sentence (1)

Ⓑ sentence (3)

Ⓒ sentence (5)

Ⓓ sentence (7)

b) The sentences in this passage are out of order. Which of the following shows the correct order of sentences?

Ⓐ 1, 3, 6, 4, 5, 2

Ⓑ 2, 5, 1, 6, 3, 4

Ⓒ 3, 4, 2, 1, 5, 6

Ⓓ 5, 6, 3, 2, 4, 1

c) Which sentence **best** represents what the passage is mainly about?

Ⓐ sentence (2)

Ⓑ sentence (3)

Ⓒ sentence (4)

Ⓓ sentence (6)

Hint #1:

The passage opening should introduce the topic **in general**.

Hint #2:

The sentences within the passage should **support** the general topic.

Answers to Challenge Activity:

a) Choice **D** is correct.

Sentence (7) does not fit into the passage. The passage discusses spider plants, but sentence (7) is talking about actual spiders.

b) Choice **B** is correct.

This passage is about spider plants. The **first** sentence tells you the **topic**. The **second** sentence tells you why it's **important**. The **remaining sentences** proceed in an **order that explains** how the spider plants send out shoots and what makes them special.

c) Choice **A** is correct.

Sentence (2) best represents what the passage is mainly about. The purpose of the passage is to let the reader know that, "**Spider plants are an amazing example of nature's intelligence**." The other sentences support this idea.

Let's take a quick test and see how much you've learned during this climb up *SCORE!* Mountain.

Good luck!

Read the passage below, then answer questions 1–3.

Note that this is a rough draft of a student essay (it contains errors).

(1) People think that history is a collection of facts. (2) That history is a collection of stories. (3) Whoever writes the stories down gets to decide the "facts" that people learn years later. (4) Even when you look at original documents, you understand them through the way you see the world. (5) Many people in history never had their stories written down. (6) History is mostly the story of rich people. (7) There are also way too many dates to memorize and it's really boring.

1. What word or words should the writer add to the beginning of sentence (2)?

(A) So

(B) The truth is

(C) Also

(D) And anyway

2. Which sentence should the writer remove from the passage?

(A) sentence (1)

(B) sentence (3)

(C) sentence (5)

(D) sentence (7)

3. The writer wants to add a new sentence to the end of the passage. Which would be the best sentence to add?

（A）Hopefully, everyone's story will be a positive part of history.

（B）But that's OK, because rich people were in charge.

（C）It's also the story of wars.

（D）So don't bother doing your homework.

Read the information below, then answer question 4.

Julio's teacher gave him an assignment to read about an issue in his town, then to write a letter to the newspaper telling how he feels about it.

4. Julio is going to write a

（A）personal letter.

（B）letter of complaint.

（C）letter to the editor.

（D）letter of request.

Read the following sentence from Julio's letter:

There needs to be a bus later in the afternoon so that kids who want to play sports have a way to get home if their parents are at work and can't pick them up from school.

5. What is Julio's letter most likely about?

（A）the need for additional bus times

（B）how great the bus system is

（C）problems parents have trying to help their kids

（D）things to do after school

Answers to test questions:

1. Choice **B** is correct.

   Changing **sentence (2)** to read, "**The truth is that history is a collection of stories**," highlights the author's goal to argue against the previous sentence, that, "People think that history is a collection of facts."

2. Choice **D** is correct.

   The writer should remove **sentence (7)** from the passage. Saying that, "**There are also way too many dates to memorize and it's really boring**," does nothing to support the author's main points.

3. Choice **A** is correct.

   Adding the sentence, "**Hopefully, everyone's story will be a positive part of history**," is a good way to end the passage on a positive note and reinforces the writer's assertion that, "**History is a collection of stories**."

4. Choice **C** is correct.

   Julio is going to write a **letter to the editor**. A letter to the editor of a newspaper usually contains a person's opinion about an issue.

5. Choice **A** is correct.

   Julio's letter is most likely about **the need for additional bus times**. His letter talks about his feelings that there should be a good way for kids who play after-school sports to get home if their parents are at work and can't pick them up. He writes, "**There needs to be a bus later in the afternoon so that kids who want to play sports have a way to get home**."

Celebrate!

Let's take a fun break before we go to the next base camp. You've earned it!

Let's have some fun with music!

Do you have a favorite band? Who is it?

Did you discover them yourself or did someone tell you about them?

Either way, it's time to turn on some music and have fun!

Congratulations!
You're getting closer to the top of *SCORE!* Mountain.

Here are some ideas:

- Turn on your stereo, or put on your favorite CD, and listen to your favorite band or singer as you take a break from studying.
- If you know how to make CDs, make a mix CD with your favorite songs!
- It's a great way to relax and unwind!

Good luck and have fun!
You deserve it for working so hard!

1. What **tense** is the verb *dug*?

(A) past

(B) present

(C) future

(D) infinitive

Hint #1:

The **infinitive form** of this word is "**to dig**."

Hint #2:

This is an **irregular verb**. That means it doesn't follow the regular rules for verbs.

Answer: Choice **A** is correct.

The word *dug* is in the past tense. The word *dig* is an **irregular verb**. To put a verb in the past tense, you usually add the letters *-ed* to the end of the word. In this case, you change the *i* to a *u*.

You just have to memorize some irregular verbs, because they don't follow any rules!

© Kaplan Publishing, Inc.

Read the following sentence, then answer question 2.

There is a slight increase in cost to support organic farming.
It preserves our land and gives us healthier food!

2. What is the **best** way to **combine** these two sentences into a single complete sentence?

    Ⓐ There is a slight increase in cost to support organic farming, and it preserves our land and gives us more healthful food!

    Ⓑ There is a slight increase in cost to support organic farming; it preserves our land and gives us more healthful food!

    Ⓒ There is a slight increase in cost to support organic farming, but it preserves our land and gives us more healthful food!

    Ⓓ There is a slight increase in cost to support organic farming, it preserves our land and gives us more healthful food!

Hint #1:

To combine sentences correctly, the new sentence should **not** be a **run-on**.

Hint #2:

One sentence says something **different** than the other. That means the sentences need to connect with a **contrast** word.

Answer: Choice **C** is correct.

The first sentence says something that people would see as a **negative**. The second sentence says something **positive**. That means the two sentences **contrast**. To connect contrasting sentences, you can use the word **but**.

3. Which answer choice **best** fills the blank in the sentence below?

The campers packed up _____ things and got ready to climb to the top of the mountain.

(A) there

(B) their

(C) they're

(D) thare

Hint #1:

The missing word describes things that **belong** to the campers.

Hint #2:

Try each answer choice in the blank. Eliminate the choices that don't fit.

© Kaplan Publishing, Inc.

Answer: Choice **B** is correct.

The campers packed up **their** things and got ready to climb to the top of the mountain. The missing word is the **possessive**: the things belong to the campers. The word **their** is the possessive meaning "**belonging to them.**"

4. Write the **plural** form of the word *goose* on the line below.

_____

Hint #1:

This is an **irregular noun**, so you **don't** add *s* to make the plural.

Hint #2:

Have you ever seen the plural form of the word *goose* written somewhere? How was it spelled?

Answer: The plural of *goose* is *geese*.

Most nouns add **s** to make the plural, but some words have their own rules. Like *mouse* (plural: *mice*), the plural of *goose* is *geese*.

Read the following passage, then answer questions 5–7.

(1) Did you ever think about where you're furniture comes from? (2) Many of the most beautiful tables, chairs, dressers, and beds are made from wood that comes from rainforests. (3) Cutting down trees in the rainforest will upset the balance of these delicate ecosystems, and will leed to the extinction of many types of animals and plants. (4) It could actually cause the biggest extinction that the world has ever seen, worse than the dinosaurs. (5) So the next time you hear the word *mahogany*, don't think "beautiful," think "endangered"

5. In sentence (1), the writer should change

(A) *you* to *I*.

(B) *think* to *thought*.

(C) *where* to *we're*.

(D) *you're* to *your*.

Hint #1:

To **whom** is the writer talking throughout the rest of the passage?

Hint #2:

Try saying the sentence with each of the changes to see which one sounds right.

Answer: Choice **D** is the correct answer.

In sentence (1), the writer should change **you're** to **your**.

The writer is asking you to think about where the things you own are made. Because the furniture the writer is talking about belongs to you, the word should be written **your**, not **you're**.

6. In sentence (3), the word *leed* should be spelled

(A) led.

(B) lead.

(C) lede.

(D) lied.

Hint #1:

The word is being used in the **future tense**.

Hint #2:

Do any of the choices seem as though they would be pronounced differently?

Answer: Choice **B** is correct.

In sentence (3), the word *leed* should be spelled *lead*.

The correct spelling of the word is *lead.* It means "**to cause**," but it can also mean "**to take charge**."

7. Sentence (5) is missing **punctuation** at the end. It should end in

(A) a period.

(B) a semicolon.

(C) an exclamation point.

(D) a question mark.

Hint:

Does this writer seem to be explaining a situation that she is excited about or trying to convince you of something?

Answer: Choice **C** is correct.

Sentence (5) is missing **an exclamation point (!)**.

The writer is excited about making her point and wants everyone to understand how important it is. The last sentence reminds you how much she cares about the issue. To reinforce the importance of her point, the last sentence should end with an exclamation point.

© Kaplan Publishing, Inc.

Read the following sentence, then answer questions 8 and 9.

Jason enjoys the heat of summer but I dont.

8. There is an **apostrophe (')** missing in this sentence. Where should it go?

Ⓐ Jason'

Ⓑ enjoy's

Ⓒ summer'

Ⓓ don't

Hint #1:

Apostrophes are used in contractions. For example, the contraction of *they will* is *they'll*.

Hint #2:

Apostrophes also can be used in **possessives**. For example, if you want to say the book that belongs to Kevin, you can say "**Kevin's book**."

Answer: Choice **D** is correct.

The word **don't** is a contraction of **do** and **not**. It needs an apostrophe and should be written as **don't**. None of the other words is a contraction or possessive, so none of them needs an apostrophe.

9. This sentence is missing a **comma**. Where should it go?

Ⓐ Jason,

Ⓑ enjoys,

Ⓒ summer,

Ⓓ but,

© Kaplan Publishing, Inc.

Hint #1:

Commas **separate** thoughts in a sentence.

Hint #2:

If the sentence is **divided** into two parts, a comma can connect them.

Answer: Choice **C** is correct.

The word **but** is a connecting word.

The two thoughts in the sentence are, "**Jason likes the heat of summer**," and "**I don't**." To link those thoughts together, you need a comma. The rule is that the comma goes **after** the last word of the first thought and **before** the connecting word.

Read the sentence below, then answer question 10.

The baseball team practice every day after school, even when it's raining.

10. In the sentence above, how should the word *practice* be written?

Ⓐ practices

Ⓑ practicing

Ⓒ was practicing

Ⓓ practiced

Hint #1:

A team is made up of a lot of people, but the word *team* is singular. A team is **one** thing.

Hint #2:

The phrase "**even when it's raining**" tells you that the sentence is written in the **present tense**.

Answer: Choice **A** is correct.

The word *team* is an example of a **collective noun**. That means it's a **singular noun** that represents **many** people or things.

The second half of the sentence tells you that it's in the present tense. The **singular present form** of the word *practice* is *practices*.

11. Which word **best** fills the blank in the sentence below?

The tree drops _____ leaves in the fall.

(A) hers

(B) it

(C) it's

(D) its

Hint #1:

The missing word is a **possessive** that tells you that the leaves belong to the tree.

Hint #2:

Trees and other plants are **not** described as male or female.

Answer: Choice **D** is correct.

The tree drops **its** leaves in the fall.

Trees are **not** described as male or female, so the pronoun to refer to trees is *it*. In this sentence, you need the **possessive** form of *it*, which is *its*.

If you wrote *it's*, that is incorrect. *It's* is the contraction of "*it is*."

Read the following sentence, then answer questions 12–14.

The last time Abby used her camera, he forgot to turn on the flash, but all her photos were two dark.

12. Which word in the sentence above should be replaced with the word *she*?

Ⓐ Abby

Ⓑ her

Ⓒ he

Ⓓ the

Hint #1:

The word *she* substitutes for the **subject** of a sentence, the one doing the action.

Hint #2:

It's easy to get lost in a sea of pronouns. Make sure we still know whom this sentence is about!

Answer: Choice **C** is correct.

The original sentence makes a mistake by referring to Abby as **both** a boy and a girl. Because Abby is usually a girl's name, and the word *her* is used in two other places in the sentence, Abby must be a **girl**. That means the word *he* needs to be changed to *she*.

13. In the sentence, the word *but* should be replaced with

(A) if

(B) when

(C) until

(D) so

Hint #1:

This is a **cause-and-effect** sentence. Because Abby forgot to turn on the flash, the photos came out badly.

Hint #2:

The replacement word should be a **connecting word**.

Answer: Choice **D** is correct.

In the sentence, the word *but* should be replaced with *so*.

The connecting word needs to be a cause-and-effect word, such as *so*.

14. In the sentence, the word *two* should be spelled

(A) to

(B) too

(C) toe

(D) three

Hint #1:

As it is used in the sentence, the word means **overly** or **excessively**.

Hint #2:

This is a word that a lot of students confuse. Look carefully!

Answer: Choice **B** is correct.

In the sentence, the word *two* should be spelled *too*.

The words *to*, *too*, and *two* are **homonyms**, which means they sound the same but are spelled differently and have different meanings. The word *too* means "**a lot**" or "**more than you need**," the meaning that fits best in this sentence.

Read the passage below, then answer questions 15–17.

(1) Some people crave adventure. (2) They like riding on roller coasters, watching scary movies, and eat unusual food. (3) For other people, happiness is in the familiar. (4) They like to be "regulars" at their favorite restaurants and bookstores. (5) For these people, feeling connected is more important than finding something new. (6) One thing that makes the world <u>intresting</u> is that both kinds of people live in it. (7) Which one is you?

15. What change should be made to sentence (2)?

Ⓐ Change *eat* to *eating*.

Ⓑ Delete the comma after *movies*.

Ⓒ Change *like* to *likes*.

Ⓓ Change *food* to *foode*.

Hint #1:

This sentence **lists** a series of items. What do you know about lists?

Hint #2:

Eliminate the answer choices that don't improve the sentence.

© Kaplan Publishing, Inc.

Answer: Choice **A** is correct.

You should change *eat* to *eating*. When you have a list, all the items in the list need to be in the **same form**. In this list, the first two items are in the **present participle**, or **-ing** form, so the third item must be in that, too.

16. What is the correct way to write sentence (7)?

(A) Which one am you?

(B) Which one are you?

(C) Which one you is?

(D) Which one you?

Hint #1:

The subject of this sentence is "**you**."

Hint #2:

Make sure the sentence has a **verb**.

Answer: Choice **B** is correct.

The correct way to write sentence (7) is: **Which one are you?**

The verb needs to match the subject. The subject in this sentence is *you*, so the verb form that matches it is *are*.

17. What is the correct way to write the **underlined word** from sentence (6)?

Ⓐ intersting

Ⓑ intristing

Ⓒ interesting

Ⓓ intrusting

Hint #1:

Try removing the *-ing* from the end of the word. What remains should make sense as a word on its own.

Hint #2:

Sometimes it's tempting to spell a word the way it sounds when you say it quickly. Make sure not to leave anything out, though!

© Kaplan Publishing, Inc.

Answer: Choice **C** is correct.

The correct spelling of this word is *interesting*. It means "**having a lot of interest.**"

136 **SCORE!** *Mountain Challenge*

Read the following sentence, then answer question 18.

J. K. rowling is such a talented writer that her *Harry Potter* series of books encouraged kids to read who never liked doing it before.

18. Which word in the sentence should be **capitalized**?

Ⓐ rowling

Ⓑ writer

Ⓒ series

Ⓓ read

Hint #1:

Always capitalize the first word in a **sentence**, **name**, and **title**.

Hint #2:

Don't use capitalization for emphasis.

Answer: Choice **A** is correct.

Rowling should be capitalized. The writer's name is **J. K. Rowling**, so it needs to be capitalized. (The initials *J. K.* stand in place of her first and middle names.) All the other choices are not being used in a name, a title, or at the beginning of a sentence.

Read the following sentence, then answer question 19.

No one was surprised when Ananda became a singer, _____ she always sang everywhere she went.

19. Which word **best** fills in the blank in the sentence above?

(A) instead

(B) because

(C) if

(D) until

Hint #1:

This is a **cause-and-effect** sentence.

Hint #2:

The missing word is a **connecting word**.

Answer: Choice **B** is correct.

No one was surprised when Ananda became a singer, because she always sang everywhere she went. The other answer choices do not fit into the sentence!

Challenge Activity

You're doing a great job so far!
Are you ready for a Challenge Activity?

Good luck!

Read the following passage, then answer the questions that follow.

when a Filmmaker puts together the soundtrack for a Movie, He tries to make it suport the story without distracting the watcher from what is hapening on the screen. when done well, the music makes the Viewer feel more conected with the story and more moved by it. Filmmaker zach braff was nomnated for awards for his choice of music in his film, Garden state.

a) **Underline** each word that should be capitalized.

b) **Circle** each word that should **not** be capitalized.

c) **Write** the misspelled words in the box below, along with their correct spellings.

Misspelled Word	Correct Spelling

See hints and answers on following page.

Hint #1:

If the word is a name or a title, it should be capitalized, and if it is a regular word, it shouldn't.

Hint #2:

Read carefully! You are not in a rush, so take your time and go at your own pace.

Answers to Challenge Activity: Did you find all the capitalization errors for parts **a** and **b**?

Below, words needing capitalization are <u>underlined</u>, and words that should be circled for removal of capitals are in **bold**.

<u>When</u> a **filmmaker** puts together the soundtrack for a **movie he** tries to make it support the story without distracting the watcher from what is happening on the screen. <u>When</u> done well, the music makes the **viewer** feel more connected with the story and more moved by it. Filmmaker <u>Zach</u> <u>Braff</u> was nominated for awards for his choice of music in his film, *Garden* <u>State</u>.

c) Did you find and correct all of the misspelled words?

Misspelled Words	Correct Spelling
suport	support
hapening	happening
conected	connected
nomnated	nominated

Let's take a quick test and see how much you've learned during this climb up *SCORE!* Mountain.

Good luck!

Read the passage below, then answer questions 1–3. (This is a rough draft of a student essay, so it may contain errors.)

(1) Imagine a famous <u>painter, do</u> you imagine that she just thinks of something amazing to paint and then sits down and makes the painting right away? (2) Actually, painters have to work very hard at what they do, and <u>it take</u> a lot of practice. (3) Painters make sketches and practice paintings and sometimes spend months getting a painting just right. (4) One painter who was famous for constantly practicing was Monet. (5) His studys of the same haystack, church, or bridge now reside in museums. (6) It's kind of funny that his homework became art themselves!

1. Which is the best way to write the underlined portion of sentence (1)?

Ⓐ painter do

Ⓑ painter. Do

Ⓒ painter "do

Ⓓ painter? Do

2. Which is the best way to write the underlined portion of sentence (2)?

Ⓐ it took

Ⓑ it taking

Ⓒ it takes

Ⓓ it's taking

3. Which word in sentence (5) is spelled incorrectly?

Ⓐ studys

Ⓑ haystack

Ⓒ reside

Ⓓ museums

4. Which change should be made to sentence (6)?

Ⓐ Add a comma after *funny*.

Ⓑ Change *art* to *Art*.

Ⓒ Delete *that*.

Ⓓ Change *themselves* to *itself*.

© Kaplan Publishing, Inc.

Read the following sentence, then answer question 5.

Those fluttering specks may seem held up by <u>magic but</u> anyone can fly a kite.

5. What is the correct way to write the underlined part of the sentence?

(A) magic; but

(B) magic: but

(C) magic, but

(D) magic. but

Answers to test questions:

1. Choice **B** is correct.
Sentence (1) should be broken up into two sentences as follows: **Imagine a famous painter. Do you imagine that she just thinks of something amazing to paint and then sits down and makes the painting right away**?

2. Choice **C** is correct.
Sentence (2) should read as follows: **Actually, painters have to work very hard at what they do, and it takes a lot of practice**.

3. Choice **A** is correct.
The word *studys* is spelled incorrectly. It should be spelled *studies*.

4. Choice **D** is correct.
Change *themselves* to *itself* in sentence (6).

5. Choice **C** is correct.
The sentence should read as follows: **Those fluttering specks may seem held up by magic, but anyone can fly a kite**.

Celebrate!

Let's take a fun break before we go to the next base camp. You've earned it!

Take a break from studying and call or instant message (IM) a friend or family member!

You can:

- Spend some time on the phone or on the Internet catching up with someone you know.
- Talk about how things are going in each of your lives and how each of you is doing.
- Fill each other in on all the latest news!

Congratulations!
You're almost to the top of *SCORE!* Mountain.

It's always nice to talk to someone you care about, and it's a great way to catch up on what's new!

Good luck and have fun! You've earned it!

Read the following letter of complaint, then answer questions 1–4.

October 16, 2006
Super Sneakers
1 Super Sneakers Way
Anytown, State 00000

To Whom It May Concern,

I recently purchased a pair of "xtra super" Super Sneakers, #XSSS1234. I love them. So I was unhappy when the laces started to fall apart after only a month. Because the laces are orange, I can't replace them at any local store.

Please send me a new pair of orange laces for my sneakers so that I can wear them again.

I have always had good experiences with the Super Sneakers Company, and I know this problem will be fixed quickly. I enclosed my store receipt and a photo of the sneakers. Thanks for your help.

Sincerely,

Max Simons

1. What did Max ask the company to do about his sneakers?

_____

_____

_____

Hint #1:

Did Max ask for something **specific** from the company?

Hint #2:

Max's request is a good one, because it tells the company **exactly** what he would like it to do to fix the problem.

Answer: Max asks **for a new pair of orange laces**, to replace the old ones that have fallen apart.

2. What **proof** does Max include to show that the problem is real?

_____

_____

© Kaplan Publishing, Inc.

Hint #1:

Remember, the company wants to make sure that Max actually owns the sneakers. They don't want to send out orange laces to anyone who asks.

Hint #2:

Proof is facts you can see.

Answer: Max includes **the store receipt and a photo of the sneakers** as proof that the problem is real.

3. Why does Max include **both** the model number and the name of his sneakers?

(A) He doesn't know which one to use.

(B) He thinks that the company might not remember the sneakers.

(C) He wants to be very clear about which sneakers he bought.

(D) He wants new sneakers, not new laces.

Hint #1:

Does Max seem as though he knows how to write a letter of complaint?

Hint #2:

In a letter of complaint, it's important to prove to the company that you have a real problem and aren't just trying to get something from the company for free.

Answer: Choice **C** is correct.

In a letter of complaint, you should always include as much information as you can. It proves to the company that your problem is real, and it helps them to solve it. The Super Sneaker Company might make several versions of the "xtra super," so Max includes both the model number and the name of his sneakers. **He wants to be very clear about which sneakers he bought.**

4. What other information should Max include in his letter?

(A) a list of other things he has bought from the Super Sneaker Company

(B) his home address

(C) his sneakers

(D) a threat to never buy their sneakers again

Hint #1:

What is Max trying to accomplish? Any new information should help him reach his goal.

Hint #2:

Are any of these choices **impractical** or **unrelated** to Max's problem?

Answer: Choice **B** is correct.

Max should include **his home address** in his letter. Max needs to include his home address so the company can send him the new laces. None of the other choices will help him get the new laces.

In a letter of complaint, it's important to be reasonable in your request. For question 5, decide on the right solution when drafting a letter for the problem presented below.

5. Your new winter boots are not waterproof as advertised.

    (A) Ask for stock in the company that makes the boots.

    (B) Ask the company to replace the boots.

    (C) Ask for a cash refund of twice the cost of the boots.

    (D) Ask for free samples of other items that the company makes.

Hint #1:

Try to figure out what is actually broken and what would fix the problem.

Hint #2:

Make sure that your proposed solution **fixes the problem**, no more and no less.

Answer: Choice **B** is correct.

Your new winter boots are not working as advertised. In your letter of complaint to the company that makes the boots, you should **ask the company to replace the boots**.

Read the following passage, then answer questions 6–8.

Have you ever called an attention-seeking friend a "drama queen"? Maybe you asked to have your meal "supersized"? Chances are, you "Google" at least a few times a week.

Merriam-Webster has just revealed its list of 100 new words that will be added to the dictionary this fall. Among those words are *unibrow* (eyebrows growing together) and *manga* (Japanese comic books). These new words address the increased range of people's information needs.

6. What event is this passage about?

Ⓐ the difference between technical terms and slang

Ⓑ the problem of words from other languages coming into English

Ⓒ why words no one has heard of are in the dictionary

Ⓓ the introduction of new words to a dictionary

Hint #1:

Look at the example words in the article. How are they **similar**?

Hint #2:

An event is a **specific thing**. What specific thing happened in the article?

Answer: Choice **D** is correct.

This passage is about **the introduction of new words to a dictionary**. Merriam-Webster, a dictionary publisher, announced the list of new words it will add to its dictionary.

7. Why do you think that Merriam-Webster would want to make a big public announcement about these updates?

_____

_____

_____

Hint #1:

Merriam-Webster is a company that produces dictionaries.

Hint #2:

What is the **business goal** of a company that produces dictionaries?

Answer: Your answer may vary. Here is a possible answer:

Merriam-Webster would want to make a big public announcement about these updates so that people buy newer versions of its dictionaries.

8. What does this passage tell you about the English language?

_____

_____

_____

_____

Hint #1:

The dictionary is a book that tries to include a definition of **every word** in the English language.

Hint #2:

The words being added to the dictionary are words that many people **already** know and use.

Answer: Your answers may vary, but this passage tells you that **the English language is always changing and growing**.

Read the following passage, then answer questions 9–11.

It seems like everyone these days is talking about **blogs**. Both kids and grown-ups are keeping blogs now, all over the country. I think it's a great way to stay in touch with friends and family who live far away, and it's fun to chat with your friends online, but I'm surprised about some of the things I read on people's blogs. I think sometimes people think of their blogs as being like their diaries. I don't know about you, but I sure wouldn't want half my school, or my parents, reading my diary.

9. What does the writer think is the **difference** between a blog and a diary?

Ⓐ Blogs are public and diaries are private.

Ⓑ Blogs are private and diaries are public.

Ⓒ Blogs are for kids and diaries are for grown-ups.

Ⓓ Blogs are for grown-ups and diaries are for kids.

Hint #1:

Where are blogs and diaries kept?

Hint #2:

What is the writer assuming about her diary?

Answer: Choice **A** is correct.

The writer of this passage thinks that **blogs are public and diaries are private**.

10. Why do you think the writer says that she wouldn't want anyone to read her diary?

_____

_____

_____

Hint #1:

Remember what the writer sees as the **difference** between a blog and a diary.

Hint #2:

The writer is **surprised** about what she reads on people's blogs.

Answer: The writer wouldn't want anyone to read her diary, because it's a private place for her to write her personal thoughts. That is why she is surprised about things she reads in people's blogs; it's information she sees as private.

11. Spend a minute now **writing down your thoughts**. It may feel a little strange if you aren't used to writing this way, but writing in a journal or diary can dramatically improve your writing skills!

_____

_____

_____

_____

_____

_____

_____

_____

_____

_____

_____

_____

Answer: Everyone's thoughts are different, so there is no right answer.

Read the passage below, then answer question 12.

We read instructions all the time. Whether we need to put together a piece of furniture, set up a new cell phone, or learn how to play a game, instructions are a part of daily life.

12. Think about something you know how to do **well**. It might be as common as making a sandwich or as unique as doing a complicated skateboarding trick. Create a set of instructions to tell someone else how to do it.

_____

_____

_____

_____

_____

_____

Hint #1:

Make sure you write the instructions in the **correct order**. You don't want someone to get up in the air for the trick before knowing how to stand on the skateboard!

Hint #2:

Make sure **not to leave out** anything important from your instructions. When you do something well, some steps might seem obvious to you, but they may not be obvious to someone trying it for the first time!

© Kaplan Publishing, Inc.

Answer: Everyone is good at different things, so everyone will choose to write about something different. There is no right answer! Just make sure that your instructions are in the right order and they don't leave out anything important! You might want to ask someone else to read your instructions and tell you if they seem complete and logical.

160 **SCORE!** *Mountain Challenge*

Read the following recipe, then answer questions 13–15.

Chocolate Chip Cookie Recipe

$2\frac{1}{4}$ cups all-purpose flour

1 teaspoon baking soda

1 teaspoon salt

1 cup (2 sticks, $\frac{1}{2}$ lb) butter, softened

$\frac{3}{4}$ cup granulated (white) sugar

$\frac{3}{4}$ cup packed brown sugar

1 teaspoon vanilla extract

2 eggs

2 cups (one 12-oz package) chocolate chips

1 cup chopped nuts

Combine flour, baking soda, and salt in a small bowl. Beat butter, granulated sugar, brown sugar, and vanilla in a large mixer bowl. Add eggs one at a time, beating well after each addition; gradually beat in flour mixture. Stir in chips and nuts. Drop by rounded tablespoons onto ungreased baking sheets.

Bake in preheated 375°F oven for 9 to 11 minutes or until golden brown. Let stand for 2 minutes; remove to wire racks to cool completely.

13. What mistake could a cook make by not reading the entire recipe before starting to make the cookies?

Ⓐ The cook might not add in the chocolate chips.

Ⓑ The cook might bake the cookies at the wrong temperature.

Ⓒ The cook might not preheat the oven first.

Ⓓ The cook might use margarine instead of butter.

Hint #1:

Is there anything that needs to be done at the very **beginning** that isn't listed at the beginning?

Hint #2:

Think about making cookies. What's the **first thing** you need to do?

Answer: Choice **C** is correct.

By following the order of the recipe instructions closely, **the cook might not preheat the oven first** before making the batter.

14. What **final instruction** might you add to this recipe?

(A) Make sure you have all your ingredients on hand before you start.

(B) You can also stir in dried fruit or other kinds of chocolate.

(C) Remember to turn off the oven when you have baked all your cookies.

(D) Let your baking sheet cool down between batches.

Hint #1:

The new instruction will come at the very **end** of the recipe, so make sure that's where it belongs.

Hint #2:

Eliminate the answer choices that don't belong at the end of the cookie recipe.

Answer: Choice **C** is correct.

Telling people to **remember to turn off the oven when you have baked all your cookies** is a good final instruction to add to this recipe. The last thing to do after cooking is to turn off the oven. All of the other instructions among the answer choices happen while the cook is still making the cookies.

15. Imagine that you are about to make this cookie recipe for your friends and have just learned that one of them is allergic to chocolate. Which is the best resource to research other cookie recipes?

(A) today's newspaper

(B) a dictionary

(C) an encyclopedia

(D) a baking Web site

Hint #1:

Which answer choice would be **most likely** to have a list of possible cookie recipes?

Hint #2:

Think of how you've used each of the items in the answer choices. Eliminate any choices that wouldn't likely have cookie recipes.

Answer: Choice **D** is correct.

The best resource to research cookie recipes would be **a baking Web site**. The Internet is a great tool for doing research. There are informative Web sites on just about any topic you can think of!

Read the sentences below, then answer questions 16–19.

You want to write a **letter to the editor** of your school newspaper. Your letter will suggest that the school use the empty patch of ground next to it as a garden.

16. You should **start** your letter with which of the following opening lines?

Ⓐ Hey guys,

Ⓑ To the editor:

Ⓒ Hi there,

Ⓓ Dear sirs,

Hint #1:

The first line of the letter talks to your audience. Who is your audience?

Hint #2:

This is a **formal** letter, not a casual one.

Answer: Choice **B** is correct.

The letter should start by saying to whom you are writing: **to the editor**.

17. The **beginning** of your letter should say what you want, as clearly and directly as possible. Try writing the first sentence of your letter in the space below.

_____

_____

_____

Hint #1:

What are you telling the editor in this letter?

Hint #2:

Make sure to write a clear, full sentence.

Answer: Everyone's answer will vary, but your first sentence should clearly discuss the purpose of your letter, such as: **The empty patch of land next to our school should be used for a garden**. Your sentence may be a little different from ours, but make sure it clearly states the reason you are writing the letter.

18. In a letter to the editor, you should include some reasons why your request is a good idea. Which sentence among the answer choices provides the **best** reason why your request is a good idea?

(A) I think it's nice to have gardens everywhere, so why not here?

(B) I mean, we could also have a basketball court.

(C) It would be good for the environment and would teach us about plants.

(D) We have a garden in our kitchen window, and we grow tomatoes.

Hint #1:

Your reason should be something that other people would agree with.

Hint #2:

In a letter to the editor, it's better to have general reasons instead of personal ones.

Answer: Choice **C** is correct.

Choice **C** says that the garden **would be good for the environment and would teach us about plants**. This sentence clearly shows how the garden will benefit the school.

© Kaplan Publishing, Inc.

19. At the end of your letter, you should include a **closing line** and your **signature**. Which is the best closing line and signature?

Ⓐ Sincerely, Harold Bloom, Grade 6

Ⓑ Love, Harry Bloom

Ⓒ peace, h.

Ⓓ Thanks, Harold from Ms. Carmola's class

Hint #1:

This is a **formal** letter, so the closing line should be formal.

Hint #2:

The closing line and signature should clearly tell readers who you are.

Answer: Choice **A** is correct.

The best closing line is: **Sincerely, Harold Bloom, Grade 6**.

The closing line should be formal, and *Sincerely* works well here. The best signature includes the writer's full name and something to show where the writer comes from. Choice A has all the necessary parts.

Challenge Activity

You're doing a great job so far!
Are you ready for a Challenge Activity?

Good luck!

Now it's time to write your own letter!

This is a **thank-you letter**. You are thanking your relative for the cookies that they sent you on your birthday.

    a) First, write your **opening**. Make sure to include the date and the opening "hello" line.

_____

_____

    b) Next, write the **body** of your letter: your thank-you note. Remember to mention what your relative gave you, how you enjoyed it, and that you appreciate the gift.

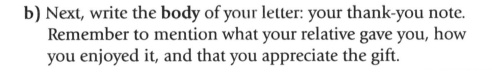

_____

_____

_____

_____

    c) Finally, finish your letter. Sign off with a **closing line** and your name.

_____

_____

_____

See hints and answers on following page.

Answer: Everyone's letter will be different! Here are some possibilities.

a) The **opening** of your letter should have today's date and whatever name you call your relative. You should use the word Dear and then his or her name, as in the example below:

> **October 15, 2006**
>
> **Dear Aunt Cathy,**

b) The **body** of your letter will sound a little different than ours but should include the same general pieces:

> **Thank you so much for the great chocolate chip cookies you sent me for my birthday! I really liked that you put white chocolate chips in them. After we ate some of them at home, I brought them in to school to share with my class. Everyone said that you are a great baker!**

c) Again, the **ending** of your letter will probably be a little different from ours, but it should have the same general parts:

> **I can't wait to come visit you this summer!**
>
> **Love,**
>
> **Kenny**

Test

Let's take a quick test and see how much you've learned during this climb up *SCORE!* Mountain.

Good luck!

Read the following passage, then answer questions 1–3.

Migratory Bird Watch

Each spring, billions of birds journey from their winter homes to summer nesting areas. On May 13, International Migratory Bird Day, bird lovers will celebrate the migration, or yearly movement.

This year, the event's spotlight is on the Boreal Forest of North America, one of the world's largest unspoiled forests. It stretches from Newfoundland, in eastern Canada, to Alaska. This forest is a nesting ground for billions of birds belonging to more than 300 species in North, Central, and South America.

Logging and development threaten the forest. The best way to save the forest is to conserve resources. Turn off lights you don't need and take a bike or bus instead of a car.

1. Why is the focus of this year's event on the Boreal Forest?

(A) It is one of the world's largest unspoiled forests.

(B) They need a new location each year.

(C) Its birds come from all over the Americas.

(D) It is threatened by logging and development.

2. International Migratory Bird Day is in May because

(A) the weather is nicest during the spring.

(B) that is when birds are migrating north.

(C) stories about the environment are published in May.

(D) it is easier to ride a bike or turn off the lights in the spring.

3. The passage suggests that people turn off lights and ride bicycles to save energy. Which answer choice is the best way for people to conserve resources?

(A) Be thoughtful of your neighbors.

(B) Go to the movies instead of watching TV.

(C) Run the air conditioner all day.

(D) Recycle paper and bottles.

Read the following passage, then answer questions 4 and 5.

March 12, 2006

Carrie Jasternak
Guide Dogs of Our State
Our Town, STATE 00000

Dear Ms. Jasternak:

My neighbor, Sandra Ellison, is a puppy raiser for Guide Dogs. She was telling me about the program, and it sounded amazing. I would like to apply to be a puppy raiser.

My family has owned dogs my whole life. We have a Labrador now, and we have had him since he was a puppy. I walk, feed, and clean him. I would feel so good about helping to get a puppy ready to be a guide dog, the most important job a dog can have.

I would be happy to come in for an interview. You can reach me any school day after 3:00 P.M. at 555-9583.

Thank you for considering my application.

Sincerely,
Jamie Samprinetti

4. Which information could Jamie include with her letter to help her get the job?

    Ⓐ A photo of her with her dog

    Ⓑ Mention of her friend's pet hamster

    Ⓒ Her summer vacation schedule

    Ⓓ The fact that she hasn't told her parents about her application

5. Which contact information should Jamie include with her letter?

    Ⓐ Her teacher's name

    Ⓑ Her nickname

    Ⓒ Her e-mail address

    Ⓓ Her parents' work phone numbers

Answers to test questions:

1. Choice **D** is correct.

According to the passage, the focus of this year's event is on the Boreal Forest **because it is threatened by logging and development**.

2. Choice **B** is correct.

International Migratory Bird Day is in May because **that is when birds are migrating north**. As stated in the passage, "Each spring, billions of birds journey from their winter homes to summer nesting areas."

3. Choice **D** is correct.

People can also **recycle paper and bottles** to conserve resources.

4. Choice **A** is correct.

Jamie is applying for a dog to be a **puppy raiser**, so she would want to show that she has experience with dogs. She could include a **photo of her with her dog** along with her letter to help show her experience.

5. Choice **C** is correct.

Jamie should include her **e-mail address** with her letter. It is a good way for her potential employer to contact her to schedule an interview.

Celebrate!

Let's have some fun and celebrate your success! You've earned it!

Let's take some of the skills you've learned and have some fun writing a short story!

What should your short story be like? That's entirely up to you!

Congratulations!
You've made it to the top of *SCORE!* Mountain. You did a great job!

SCORE! MOUNTAIN TOP

BASE CAMP 6

BASE CAMP 5

BASE CAMP 4

BASE CAMP 3

BASE CAMP 2

BASE CAMP 1

Use your imagination to create the plot, the characters, the setting, and the dialog.

Every single detail is up to you!

Even the length of your story is your decision!

You can write your story in just a few paragraphs, or you can use several pages if you like!

You can even write several stories! The more you write, the more your writing skills will improve!

When you're finished, share your story with whomever you'd like!

You should be really proud!
I knew you could make it to the top!

Here are some helpful tools to guide you through each base camp!

Use these tools whenever you need a helping hand during your climb up *SCORE!* Mountain.

Prefixes, Suffixes, and Root Words

Here is a chart of common prefixes and their meanings:

Prefix	Meaning	Sample Word
co-	with	coexist
de-	opposite	defrost
dis-	not	disagree
extra-	outside	extracurricular
in- im-	in	infield implode
mis-	wrongly	misplace
non-	not	nonsense
over-	over	overlook
pre-	before	prefix
re-	again	return
trans-	across	transport
un-	not	unfriendly

Here is a chart of common suffixes and their meanings:

Suffix	Definition	Example
-able -ible	can be done	comfortable, collectible
-er -or	one who	worker actor
-est	comparative	biggest
-ful	full of	careful
-less	without	fearless
-ous -eous -ious	possessing the qualities of	joyous righteous furious

Here is a chart of common word roots and their meanings:

Root	Meaning	Sample Word
auto	self	automatic
bene	well good	benefit
bio	life	biography
centi	hundred	centipede
chron	time	chronology
contra	against	contrary
dict	say speak	dictate
duct	lead	conduct
form	shape	formulate
fract	break	fracture
geo	earth	geology
hemi	half	hemisphere
macro	large	macroclimate
micro	small	microscope
mono	single	monorail
ology	study of	biology

Chart continued from previous page:

Root	Meaning	Sample Word
psych	mind soul	psychiatry
sphere	ball	spherical
struct	build	construct
tele	from afar	telephone
therm	heat	thermometer

Types of Figurative Language

Alliteration: The repetition of beginning word sounds, usually consonant sounds, in two or more neighboring words or syllables.

Assonance: The resemblance or repetition of vowel sounds in words or syllables.

Cliché: A phrase, expression, or idea that has become overly familiar or commonplace.

Hyperbole: An exaggeration used for emphasis.

Idiom: A word or phrase with a meaning that is known only through conventional use among a particular group of people.

Metaphor: Comparing two things by suggesting a likeness between them, without using the words *like* or *as*.

Onomatopoeia: A word that sounds like the sound it represents.

Personification: Giving human characteristics to nonhuman things.

Simile: A comparison between two things using the words *like* or *as*.

The 5 Steps of the Writing Process

Step 1: Brainstorming—thinking about and gathering ideas for what to write.

Step 2: Researching—gathering information about whom or what you are writing about.

Step 3: Writing—writing down all of your ideas.

Step 4: Revising—looking over your writing to make sure it is just the way you want it.

Step 5: Proofreading—fixing any mistakes in your writing, including grammar and facts, to make sure that your writing is as correct as possible.

The 4 Essential Parts of a Story

Step 1: Exposition (Beginning)—the beginning of the story. This is the part in which the author introduces the characters and describes the setting.

Step 2: Plot Build-Up—during this part of the story, most of the action happens. During this part, the excitement builds and the plot gets more complicated.

Step 3: Climax—this is the most exciting part of the story. This is the part where the characters face their final challenge, or finally get where they were trying to go. This is the part of the story where, when you get to it while you are reading, it's hard to put down the book.

Step 4: Dénouement (Ending)—the ending of the story, where everything gets wrapped up, and all of the questions are answered.

You can do it!

Use these blank pages to work out the questions in your
SCORE! Mountain Challenge Workbook.

You can do it!

You can do it!

You can do it!

You can do it!

You can do it!

You can do it!

You can do it!

You can do it!

You can do it!

You can do it!

You can do it!

You can do it!

You can do it!

You can do it!